WAFER PAPER Cakes

STEVI AUBLE

Modern Cake Designs and Techniques for
Wafer Paper Flowers and More

DAVID & CHARLES

www.davidandcharles.com

CONTENTS

Cakes

INTRODUCTION

Wafer paper has long been a staple product in the realm of confectionery arts, most notably in the process of nougat making. In centuries past it was considered a dessert only fit for aristocracy and the upper middle class as it was made from potatoes, a high-value commodity at the time. It has since taken on a multitude of uses and, as its main ingredients have become far more readily available, it has transformed into a very cost effective edible decorating tool. Wafer paper is light in appearance and in weight, making it a versatile medium for cake decorating that can be used *en masse* without compromising the structure of the cakes it is placed on.

In the following pages I will show you how to create a large array of wafer paper innovations from leaves to tetrahedrons, and from basic "paper" like blossoms to blooms so realistic that they are hard to differentiate from their real counterparts. You will find full instructions for making toppers proper for numerous occasions that are light, airy and quick to assemble; impressive decorative finishes like leather and edible gold sheets, and wreaths, bows and confetti that make expeditious and clever embellishments which can be used over and over. In short, I hope you will find enough practical advice and inspiration here to make you a wafer paper creator, and set you on your own path to discovering just how versatile this simple product can be.

EQUIPMENT & MATERIALS

Some of the equipment and materials required to create the various flowers, decorations and cake projects in this book are listed below and pictured opposite, from left to right and top to bottom. There are a few other essentials including edible glues, as well as a hot glue gun to attach wire to silicone shapes, and each project begins with a list of everything you'll need to make it.

- White and green cloth-covered floral wire, in various gauges
- Shell and blade modeling tool
- Wire cutters (needle-nose pliers are also useful)
- Paper Potion, edible paper conditioner
- Painter's (masking) tape, narrow
- Closed-cell styrofoam balls and cones, in varying sizes with floral wire attached (using a hot glue gun)
- Closed-cell styrofoam ball
- Styrofoam cone (egg and ball shapes also required)
- Hexagon cookie cutter (or paper punch)
- Craft fringe scissors
- White and green floral tape
- Foam brush
- Large rolling pin
- Small rolling pin
- Ruler (a clear ruler and fabric tape measure are also needed)
- Large fluffy brush
- Flat head paint brushes, in varying widths, soft and bristled
- Pencil
- Silicone round (petal) molds (silicone mold trays also required)

- Scissors
- Embossing wheel
- Vodka (or other clear high-alcohol-content liquid)
- Piping gel
- Black gel color (various other colors also needed)
- Gold highlighter dust (you'll need gold glitter too)
- Black gumpaste (white and pale green also required)
- Edible paint, in various colors
- Craft knife
- Circle paper punch (varying sizes required)
- Isomalt nibs
- Multi-star paper punch
- Fondant
- Hole punch
- Small leaf punch
- Extruder tool
- All-over-the-page paper punch
- Edible gold leaf on transfer sheets
- Petal dust (various colors needed)
- Two-sided silicone leaf veiner
- Wafer paper, in various thicknesses (you'll need wafer paper cardstock too)

COLORING & PRINTING

There are a multitude of ways to color wafer paper and each technique will yield a different effect. These four techniques are a few of the simplest and most effective for the projects in this book.

Edible printing

My go-to, and favorite, method for coloring wafer paper is to use an edible printer. An edible printer allows you to have complete control of the color results. It is also the only one of the following techniques that will give you a solid, consistent, even, overall colored sheet. There are numerous products on the edible image/printing market and all it takes to find one that works for you is to do a little research. It is important to know the products that are available in your area as well as the ones that follow your local laws and regulations. Once you have a machine that works for your needs, you can use any simple program to create a full sheet of color. I like to use Microsoft Word and simply "insert" a rectangular shape that encompasses the full page and then "fill" it with my color of choice. The paper is designed to be printed on the smooth (front) side; however, If a deeper color is desired, both sides of the paper can be printed on.

Dry petal dusts

Petal dusts can be brushed onto the smooth (front) side of the wafer paper. This is a very quick and easy coloring method that will give you a light, airy, watercolor finish. Brushing on the color in a small circular motion is the best method to disperse the petal dust. This can be done prior to assembling a flower or used as additional decoration afterwards depending on the over all look that is preferred.

Oil based colors

Edible oil based paints can be used to color wafer paper without the risk of dissolving the paper like water based colors can. There are many ready mixed colors on the market but you can also make your own by mixing a small amount of oil such as Flo-Coat, vegetable oil or shortening (white vegetable fat), with petal dust or a small amount of gel paste color. Simply mix together your dust with your oil base of choice to a medium consistency. Then brush the color onto the smooth (front) side of the paper in long smooth strokes. Once the page is full of color, set it aside to dry. Depending on the oil base used, dry time can take anywhere from a couple of hours to 24 hours plus. This method will give you a deeper tone and finish of color but will still have some streaking and inconsistency. This typically happens because the oil will soak into the paper in different areas at different rates, as well as accenting the naturally occurring imperfections within the paper.

Edible paints

This method will yield the most consistent finish next to the edible printer. Edible paints are specially formulated to work on various edible surfaces including wafer paper. It only takes a small amount brushed onto the smooth (front) side of the sheet to saturate it with color. It is also a quicker drying product than oil based paints, so paper colored in this way can be painted and used within 20 or 30 minutes.

Flowers

BASIC FLOWERS:

Paper Rose

You will find that you return to this rose again and again in your designs, so it's a great idea to master it.

YOU WILL NEED

- AD-0 wafer paper
- Pencil
- Scissors
- Gumpaste, white
- Piping gel
- Paint brush

1. Place the wafer paper on top of the paper rose templates (see Templates) and trace out five large petals, four medium petals and three small petals. Using scissors, cut out each petal. Then cut a slit into the base of each one to approximately halfway up the petal.

2. Next create the backing for the rose by taking a small amount of white gumpaste and shaping a disc with your fingers to approximately 1in (2.5cm) in diameter and ¼in (5mm) in thickness. Set aside while you prepare your petals for assembly.

3. First place all five of the largest petals upside down (rough side of the paper up) and brush a small amount of piping gel over the entirety of each petal.

4. Once all of the petals are covered in piping gel, pick them up one by one with the front (dry side) facing you and roll back the top edges of the petals to shape them. Then cross the right side of the slit over the left, creating an overlap at the base of the petal. That overlap should create a slight cupping effect.

5. After all five of your large petals are curled and cupped, place them on the gumpaste backing, one by one, overlapping them until they are placed around the circumference of the backing disc.

6. Next, repeat steps 4 and 5 for the four medium petals, and again for the three small petals until your flower is complete.

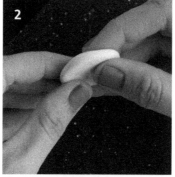

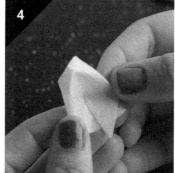
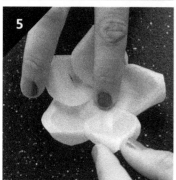

BASIC FLOWERS:

Rolled Rose

This is the simplest rose to create, which makes it a good choice if you need a lot of roses! You can make it loose and open or tight and bud-like.

YOU WILL NEED

- Gumpaste, white
- AD-0 wafer paper
- Scissors
- Piping gel
- Paint brush

1. Make a backing for your rolled rose by shaping a small piece of gumpaste into a disc that is approximately 1in (2.5cm) in diameter and ¼in (5mm) in thickness. Set this disc aside.

2. Cut the wafer paper into an 8 x 8in (20 x 20cm) square. Starting at one corner of the square, begin to cut a wavy spiral through the square, moving inwards towards the center. Once at the center leave a small open hole.

3. Once cut, place the wafer paper spiral upside down (rough side up) and brush a small amount of piping gel over the entire surface of the spiral.

4. Pick up the outside tail of the spiral with the smooth, non-piping-gel side towards you. Begin to roll the paper onto itself. As you roll, the piping gel should be on the outside.

5. Gently continue to roll the paper around itself making sure to not force or pull the paper too tight.

6. Once you have rolled the entire spiral, immediately press the bottom of the flower into the gumpaste backing to secure it.

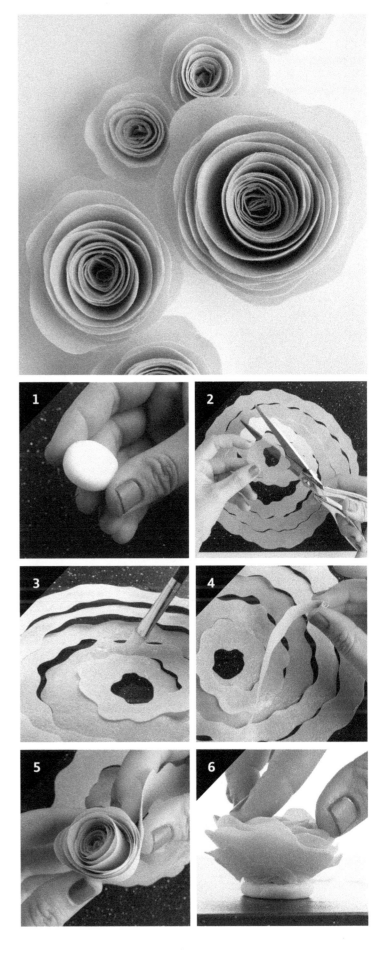

BASIC FLOWERS:

Ranunculus

This is a simple version of a ranunculus flower, which complements an arrangement of roses beautifully.

YOU WILL NEED

- Gumpaste, white
- AD-0 wafer paper
- Circle paper punches in sizes: 1in (2.5cm), 1¼in (3cm) and 1½in (4cm)
- Scissors
- Piping gel
- Paint brush

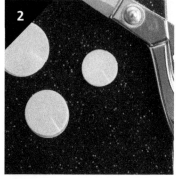

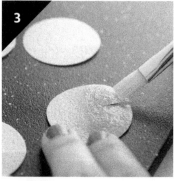

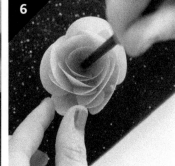

1. With a small amount of gumpaste, create a backing for your flower by using your fingers to shape a disc that is 1½in (4cm) diameter and ⅛in (3mm) in thickness. Set aside while you begin to create the petals.

2. Using the paper punches, punch out three 1in (2.5cm) petals, four 1¼in (3cm) petals and nine 1½in (4cm) petals from the wafer paper. Once the petals have been punched out, cut a ⅛in slit into all of them with scissors.

3. Starting with five of the 1½in (4cm) petals, place them upside down (rough side up) and apply a small amount of piping gel to the bottom half of all of the petals where the slit is cut.

4. Cup each petal by folding the right side of the slit over the left. Press gently together to secure.

5. Place the petals on the outer edge of the gumpaste backing, overlapping each time you place one down. If you can't place the petals with your fingers, the end of a paint brush works as a great tool to secure them. Once all five petals are placed, the outer edge of gumpaste should be completely covered.

6. Repeat steps 4 and 5 for the four remaining 1½in (4cm) large petals, placing them just inside the already-placed petals. Do the same for the 1¼in (3cm) petals, and then the 1in (2.5cm) petals, until your flower is full and complete.

BASIC FLOWERS:

Pinwheel

While the "pinwheel" is not a naturally occurring flower, it's fanned, floral shape adds a unique and interesting texture to your floral designs and it's remarkably simple to create.

YOU WILL NEED

- Gumpaste, white
- Ruler
- Pencil
- AD-00 wafer paper (color of choice)
- Scissors
- Flat-bristled paint brush
- Piping gel

1. Create a backing for your pinwheel by shaping a small piece of gumpaste into a 1in (2.5cm) diameter circle with a ¼in (5mm) thickness. Set aside.

2. Using a ruler and pencil, mark two strips of wafer paper, each measuring 1¼in (3cm) wide by 8½in (22cm) long. Cut both strips out.

3. Holding one strip of wafer paper in your fingers, fold the paper back and forth like an accordion in approximately ¼in (5mm) increments. Repeat with the second strip of wafer paper.

4. Next, prepare the gumpaste backing circle by applying a small amount of piping gel to the entire top surface. Once you have applied the piping gel, attach one accordion fold by creating a fan shape covering half of the backing. Press down firmly to secure.

5. Repeat step 4 with the second accordion fold, creating a complete circle; be sure to press firmly at the center of the pinwheel to ensure both folds are completely adhered to the gumpaste backing.

6. You may add embellishments such as pearls or dragees to the center using a small dab of piping gel.

ROSES:

Garden Rose

Soft, delicate, romantic – the appeal of the garden rose is timeless.

YOU WILL NEED

- AD-0 wafer paper
- Circle paper punches in sizes: 1½in (4cm), 1¾in (4.5cm), 2in (5cm) and 2½in (6.5cm)
- Scissors
- Silicone round molds in sizes: 1½in (4cm), 1¾in (4.5cm), 2in (5cm) and 2½in (6.5cm)
- Paper Potion, edible paper conditioner
- Water
- 1½in (4cm) closed-cell styrofoam ball, with 20-gauge green floral wire attached
- Petal dust, pale shrimp
- Paint brush

1. Punch out eight 1½in (4cm) petals, nine 1¾in (4.5cm) petals, five each of the 2in (5cm) and 2½in (6.5cm) petals with the circle punches. Trim the edge of each of the petals to give them some texture, going approximately a quarter of the way around with your scissors.

2. Place the 1½in (4cm) petals upside down (rough side up) and lightly spray with Paper Potion. Allow the potion to soak into the petals. Once the petals are pliable, place them rough side up into a round mold that is the same diameter size as the petal. Leave approximately ⅛–¼in (3–5mm) of the trimmed side of the petal above the edge of the mold. Press down to create a cupped petal, then remove from the mold. Repeat for all of the petals.

3. Once the petals are all cupped, start to form the flower by taking the styrofoam ball with the wire attached and sandwiching two of the 1½in (4cm) petals around it. The petal edges should meet at the top and hide the styrofoam ball completely. Adhere the petals to the styrofoam with a small amount of water.

4. Repeat step 3 with two more of the 1½in (4cm) petals, this time overlapping the seams of the previously placed petals and leaving a small gap at the top of the flower. Secure the petals with a small amount of water at the base.

5. Next, apply two more rows of two 1½in (4cm) petals, overlapping the seams created by the previous petals. Add a small amount of water at the base of the rose if needed to secure them.

6. Continue on to the 1¾in (4.5cm) petals starting with a row of three petals, and then overlapping with a row of four petals. Add water to adhere petals as needed.

7. Next, add a row of all five 2in (5cm) petals. It may be helpful at this point to turn your flower upside down while attaching petals, this will help to prevent any petals from drooping too far away from the flower.

8. Once that row is attached, place the five final 2½in (6.5cm) petals around the flower making sure to overlap the seams of the previously placed row. Continue adding water at the base of the petals as needed to secure them. Once attached, place the flower upside down and allow to dry for 12–24 hours.

9. After the flower is completely dry, accentuate the petals by adding a light dusting of the pale shrimp petal dust to the outer petal edges with a soft brush.

10. At the center of the flower, add multiple coats of the petal dust to deepen the color and add more depth to the garden rose.

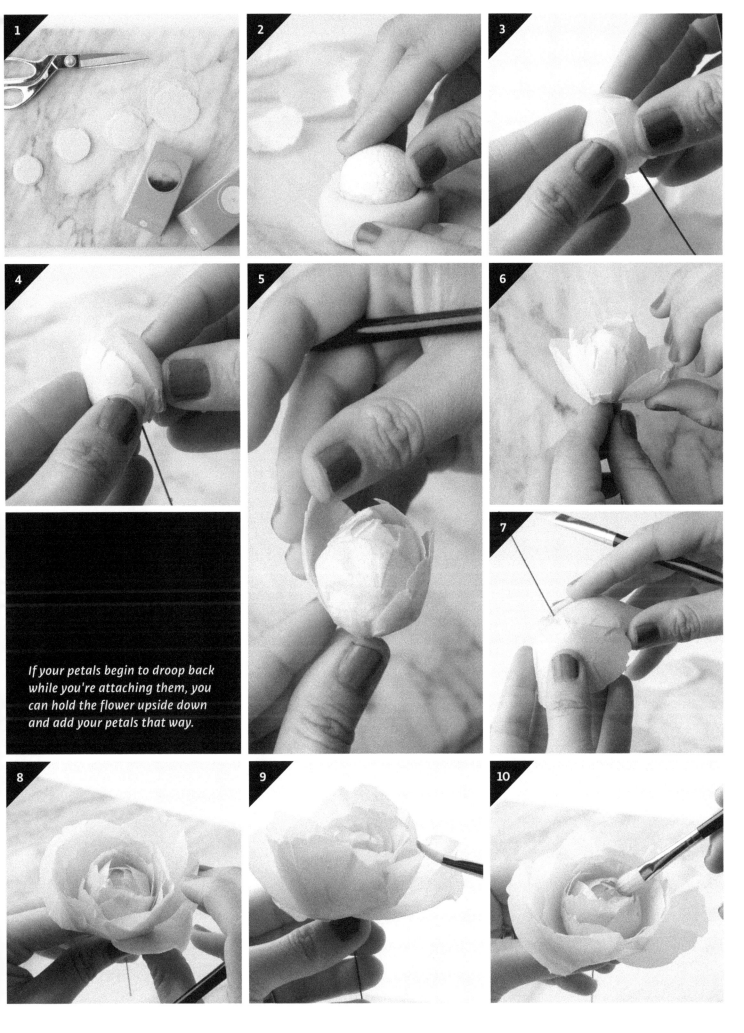

If your petals begin to droop back while you're attaching them, you can hold the flower upside down and add your petals that way.

ROSES:

Standard Rose

The standard rose is the most common and recognizable of all the roses, and is a great universal flower to use for all designs.

YOU WILL NEED

- AD-0 wafer paper
- Circle paper punches in sizes: 1⅛in (4cm), 1¾in (4.5cm) and 2in (5cm)
- Scissors
- Paper Potion, edible paper conditioner
- 1in (2.5cm) styrofoam egg, ¾in (2cm) diameter, with 20-gauge green floral wire attached
- Paint brush
- Water
- Petal dust, pink

1. Punch out twelve 1⅛in (4cm) petals, six 1¾in (4.5cm) petals and nine 2in (5cm) petals with the circle punches. Trim the edge of each of the petals, going approximately a third of the way around with your scissors, and giving them small waves and undulations. Cut a small slit, approximately ⅓in (1cm) long, directly opposite the trimmed edge of each petal. You can cut slits in multiple petals at the same time by stacking them together.

2. Place all of the 1⅛in (4cm) trimmed petals upside down (rough side facing up) and lightly spray with Paper Potion. Allow the potion to saturate the petals for approximately 60–90 seconds, or until pliable. Then pick them up one by one with the smooth side facing you and curl back the trimmed edges, creating almost a pointed end.

3. Next lay three petals, with the curl facing the egg, in a concentric circle around the styrofoam egg. They should fit tightly, overlapping one another and covering the entirety of the top of the egg. Secure the petals to the egg by applying water to the outside of the petals.

4. Once the center petals are placed, create three more rows with the 1⅛in (4cm) petals. Each row should consist of three petals. Wrap them around the previously placed petals, tacking each petal down every time they are placed with a small amount of water.

5. After all of the 1⅛in (4cm) petals are added, set the flower aside. Lay all of the 1¾in (4.5cm) petals upside down and lightly spray with Paper Potion. Allow the potion to saturate the petals for approximately 60–90 seconds, and then begin to attach them to the flower. You will create two rows of three petals. When placing the petals, make sure they are applied with the smooth side facing the inside of the flower and that they are covering up the seam between the previously placed petals. Attach each petal with a small amount of water at its base. Note that these petals will look a bit more open than the 1⅛in (4cm) petals, as they are not curled.

Due to the way the petals are trimmed and the unique nature of wafer paper in general, each of the roses you create will naturally look different from one another, which only adds to their realism.

6. To apply the 2in (5cm) petals, lay all of them upside down and lightly spray with Paper Potion, again allowing 60–90 seconds for the potion to soak into the paper. Then apply each petal with the smooth side facing the interior of the flower by overlapping the previous seams and using water to secure. There will be three rows of the 2in (5cm) petals to complete the flower. Set upside down to dry for 12–24 hours.

7. Once fully dry, run a paint brush with a light coating of pink petal dust over the edge of all of the outer petals.

8. Brush a heavier layer of pink petal dust at the center of the flower to accentuate it and add depth.

ROSES:

David Austin Rose

The distinctive petal structure of this rose makes it an impressive flower to create and use in your designs. While it looks challenging, it actually comes together quite easily.

YOU WILL NEED

- AD-0 wafer paper
- Circle paper punches in sizes: 1in (2.5cm), 1¼in (3cm), 1½in (4cm), 1¾in (4.5cm), 2½in (6.5cm) and 3in (7.5cm)
- Scissors
- Paper Potion, edible paper conditioner
- Silicone round molds in sizes: 1in (2.5cm),

1¼in (3cm), 1½in (4cm), 1¾in (4.5cm), 2½in (6.5cm) and 3in (7.5cm)
- Five pieces of 22-gauge green cloth-covered floral wire, 6in (15cm) in length
- Water
- Green floral tape
- Paint brushes
- Petal dust, aubergine

1. Using the circle paper punches, punch out ten each of all the sizes of petals: 1in (2.5cm), 1¼in (3cm), 1½in (4cm), 1¾in (4.5cm), 2½in (6.5cm) and 3in (7.5cm). Using scissors, cut small waves and undulations around a third of the circumference of all of the circles.

2. Next place all ten of the 1in (2.5cm) petals upside down (rough side facing up) and lightly spray with Paper Potion. Allow the potion to saturate the petals for approximately 60–90 seconds, or until pliable. Once pliable, individually place each petal (smooth side up) into the corresponding sized silicone round mold and press to create a cupped petal. Repeat with all of the remaining petals.

3. Once all the petals are cupped, attach one of the 1in (2.5cm) petals by dipping a 22-gauge green cloth-covered wire in water and folding the petal in thirds around the wire. Press at the base to flatten and secure the petal to the wire.

4. Proceed with one more 1in (2.5cm) petal and two rows each of the 1¼in (3cm) and 1½in (4cm) petals, placing them one by one around the previous petals and securing each one with small amount of water at the base. Pinch at the base each time to ensure they are attached to one another and secure.

5. Next take two of the 1¼in (3cm) petals and place them on either side of the center, sandwiching the center between them. Repeat steps 3–5 to create a total of five center pieces. Set aside to dry for 2–3 hours.

6. Once the centers are dry, cluster all five of them together and bind them with green floral tape. Wind the tape all the way down to the end, covering all of the wires.

7. Begin filling the flower in by attaching two rows of the 2½in (6.5cm) petals around the newly bound center with a small amount of water at the base of the petals. Using this method, place five of the petals around the center and then overlap with the next row of five petals. Repeat, this time with two rows of the 3in (7.5cm) petals. Once all of the petals are attached, place the flower upside down and allow it to dry for 12–24 hours.

8. Once fully dry, run a paint brush with a light coating of aubergine petal dust over the edge of all of the outer petals. Add a heavier coat of dust to accentuate the center of the flower.

If you find any large gaps or spaces between your petals once the flower is assembled, you can punch out a few more petals. Spray to shape the petals and then place them into the gaps, using water to secure them.

Ranunculus

The ranunculus is known for its rose-like structure of delicate but lavish petals placed in concentric rings. It is the perfect choice for a romantic cake for a wedding, anniversary or birthday if you are looking for a modern and unexpected floral option. These flowers make a big impact displayed simply on their own or complement just about any other floral arrangement, making them a versatile addition to your wafer paper flower repertoire.

YOU WILL NEED

- Flat-bristled paint brush, ½in (1cm)
- 1in (2.5cm) closed-cell styrofoam ball
- 22-gauge white cloth-covered floral wire, 6in (15cm) in length
- Hot glue gun
- Circle paper punches in sizes: 1in (2.5cm), 1¼in (3cm), 1½in (4cm) and 2in (5cm)
- Two sheets of AD-00 wafer paper

- Paper Potion, edible paper conditioner
- Silicone round molds in sizes: ¾in (2cm), 1in (2.5cm), 1¼in (3cm) and 1½in (4cm)
- Water
- Two flat-bristled paint brushes, ¼in (5mm)
- Petal dust: moss green and pink

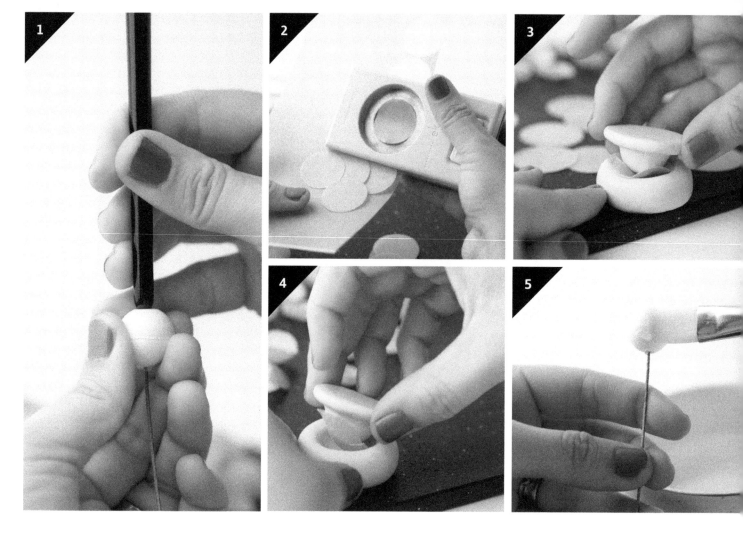

1. First prepare the ranunculus center: hot glue the wire to the styrofoam ball. Once the glue is dry, firmly press the end of a ½in (1cm) paint brush into the top center of the ball creating a small indentation.

2. Using the circle paper punches, cut out 20 petals in each of the following sizes (60 petals in total): 1in (2.5cm), 1¼in (3cm) and 1½in (4cm). Then cut ten 2in (5cm) petals. Place all the 1in (2.5cm) petals upside down (rough side up), and spray with Paper Potion according to the directions on the bottle. Allow the Potion to soak into the petals for 60–90 seconds.

3. Once the 1in (2.5cm) petals have been conditioned, shape them using the ¾in (2cm) silicone round molds. Place one petal, rough side up, in between the base and top half of the mold, then press firmly to cup the petal. Remove and continue with remaining conditioned petals.

4. Repeat steps 3 and 4 for all remaining petal sizes, using the 1in (2.5cm) mold for the 1¼in (3cm) petals, the 1¼in (3cm) mold for the 1½in (4cm) petals and the 1½in (4cm) mold for the 2in (5cm) petals.

5. Apply a small amount of water to the styrofoam ranunculus center.

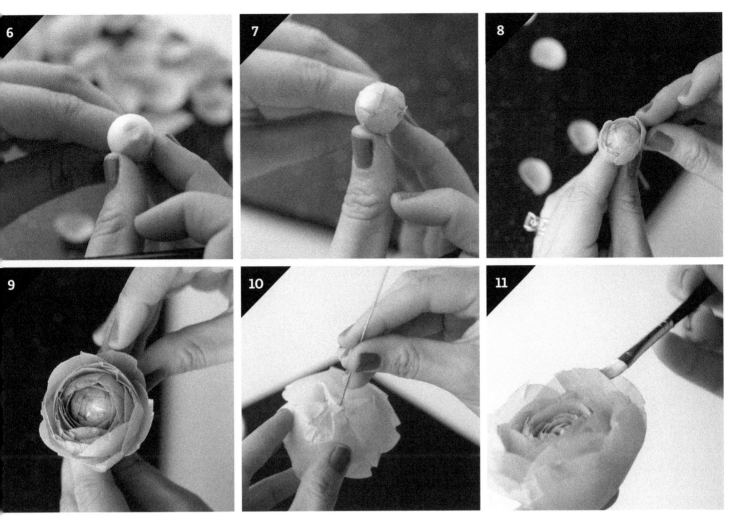

6. Starting with a 1in (2.5cm) cupped petal, place it onto the styrofoam center by positioning the edge of the petal over the middle of the indentation. Apply a small amount of water at the base of the petal to secure.

7. Repeat step 7 with two additional petals, overlapping each one. The three petals should cover the sides of the styrofoam, creating a triangular shape at the top of the ball, and the small indentation should still be slightly visible at the center.

8. Continue to apply the 1in (2.5cm) petals, overlapping each one and securing with a small amount of water at the base of each petal.

9. Once all of the 1in (2.5cm) petals are applied, repeat step 9 to attach all of the 1¼in (3cm) petals, and then the 1½in (4cm) petals.

10. Next apply the 2in (5cm) petals with a small amount of water, making sure that the bottom edge of the petal is set against the wire, covering up all of the styrofoam ball. Once all petals are affixed, place the flower upside down to dry for 2–3 hours or until firm.

11. When dry and firm to the touch, enhance the center of the flower by adding a small amount of moss green petal dust with a ¼in (5mm) flat-bristled paint brush. Highlight the edges of the petals by scraping the rim of each petal with another ¼in (5mm) flat-bristled paint brush that has a small amount of pink petal dust on it.

Peony

As one of the most popular wedding flowers, peonies have long been a staple in the cake decorating world. Re-creating this timeless flower with wafer paper allows the designer to capture their soft, airy quality without sacrificing the classic silhouette they are so well known for.

YOU WILL NEED

- Gumpaste, pale green
- Tylose glue
- Three pieces of 22-gauge green floral wire, 5in (12.5cm) in length
- Shell and blade modeling tool
- Foam block
- AD-0 wafer paper
- Scissors
- Embossing wheel
- Paper Potion, edible paper conditioner, in a spray container

- 2in (5cm) silicone round mold
- 40 pieces of 32-gauge white cloth-covered floral wire, 5in (12.5cm) in length
- Bowl of water
- Green floral tape
- Long-pointed dull white tip stamens, 1 bundle
- Petal dust: moss green, yellow and apricot
- Flat paint brush

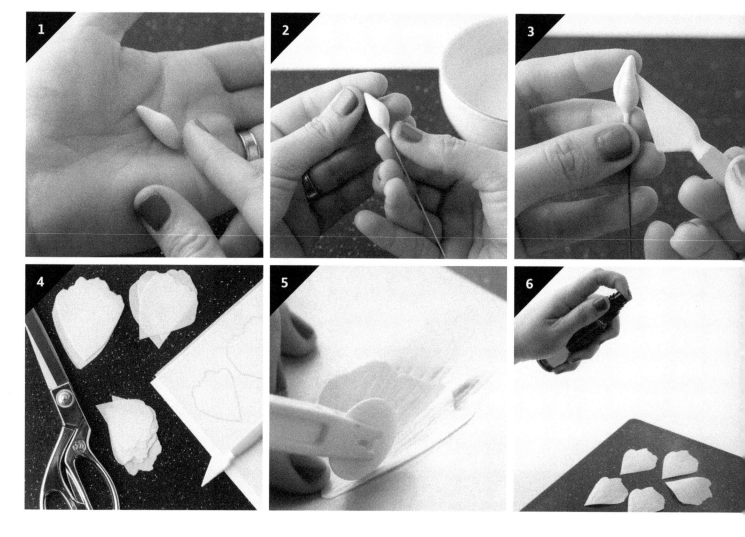

1. Create the first of the three pistils by rolling a small amount of pale green gumpaste between your finger and palm into the shape of a teardrop, approximately ½in (1cm) in length.

2. After dipping the end of a 22-gauge green floral wire into Tylose glue, insert it into the ball-end of the gumpaste teardrop and push up into the narrow end. Pinch tightly where the gumpaste and wire meet to create a smooth transition between the two.

3. Next use the blade end of the shell and blade tool to create three long indentations that extend up the length of the pistil and are evenly spaced apart. Set the wire, pistil side up, into a foam block to dry. Create two more pistils by following steps 1–3. All three pistils should be left to dry for at least 24 hours.

4. To create the petals, start by placing the wafer paper on top of the peony templates (see Templates) and trace around them with the pointed end of the shell and blade tool. Trace and cut out 15 each of the small and medium-sized petals, and ten of the large.

5. Once all of the petals are cut out, create veins in them by placing each petal smooth side up on top a scrap piece of wafer paper. Roll the embossing wheel over the surface in a fanned pattern from the bottom tip out over the end of the petal.

6. Working in batches, place five petals veined-side down on your work surface and lightly mist with Paper Potion.

7. Let the Paper Potion soak into the petals for 60–90 seconds. Once saturated, place them one by one, veined side up, into the 2in (5cm) silicone round mold. Press the ball down to cup the petals into shape, remove from the mold and then set aside to dry. Repeat steps 6 and 7 for all of the petals.

8. Next, attach 32-gauge wire to each petal by dipping approximately 1½in (4cm) of the end of the wire into a bowl of water. Wipe any excess water off the wire and then immediately place it on the reverse side of the petal, pressing and shaping the wire to attach it to the curve of the petal. Drape over the edge of a foam block to dry for approximately 1–2 hours.

9. While the petals are drying, dust each of the three pistils with a small amount of moss green petal dust, brushing from the wire up around the base, then with a small amount of yellow from the tip down. The two colors should gradually blend into one another when applied this way. You can use the same brush to apply both colors.

10. Tape the three pistils together with green floral tape and then insert into the center of the bundle of long-pointed dull white tip stamens.

11. Begin to tape the petals to the center by starting with the smallest petals first. Each row of petals placed around the center should be in increments of five. You will have three rows each of the small and medium petals, and two rows of the large outer petals.

12. To complete the flower, dust a small amount of apricot petal dust on the edges of each of the petals by dragging a flat paint brush loaded with dust over the entire edge of all the petals.

Dahlia

With their large and abundant petals, dahlias are a graceful and versatile flower. They are capable of making both a bold statement on their own, or a delicate focal point in an arrangement.

YOU WILL NEED

- AD-0 wafer paper
- Shell and blade modeling tool
- Scissors
- Embossing wheel
- Gumpaste, white
- Ruler

- Paper Potion, edible paper conditioner, in a spray container
- Water
- Paint brush
- Petal dust, peach and moss green

1. Place the wafer paper over the dahlia templates (see Templates), and trace the petals out with the blade side of the shell and blade tool. You will need to trace and cut out 12 mini petals, 12 small petals, 16 medium petals and 20 large petals.

2. When all the petals are cut out, create a veined effect by placing them one by one, front (smooth) side up, atop a scrap piece of wafer paper. Run the embossing wheel lengthwise over the petal multiple times, until the lines are abundant and visible.

3. Next create a backing for the flower by shaping a small amount of white gumpaste into a circle that is approximately 2in (5cm) in diameter and ⅛in (3mm) thick. Set the backing circle aside while you prepare the first row of petals.

4. Start by placing ten of the largest petals upside down (veining should be face down), and spray lightly with Paper Potion. Allow the potion to soak into the petals for 60–90 seconds, or until very pliable, before moving on to the next step.

5. Once the petals are saturated, place them one by one onto the outer ¼in (5mm) edge of the gumpaste backing circle. As you place each petal, pinch and roll it to shape as you secure it to the circle. If needed, use a small touch of water to adhere the petals.

6. When all ten petals are placed, they should fit snugly around the circle with the gumpaste only visible at the very center of the backing circle.

7. Repeat steps 4–5 with the remaining ten large petals. When they are ready to be placed onto the gumpaste circle, position and fix them in the gaps between the existing row of petals.

8. Next, lay eight of the medium petals upside down (veined side should be facing down) and spray them with Paper Potion, again letting it soak it into the petals for 60–90 seconds or until pliable. Pinch and roll the petals to shape as you place them in between the gaps of the previous row of petals.

9. Repeat step 8 with all 12 of the small petals. These should create two rows, consisting of six petals each.

10. Once the small petals are in place, repeat step 8 with the 12 mini petals. It is helpful, as the petals start to fill the center, to use the end of your paint brush to secure them. Set your completed flower aside to dry for 24 hours.

11. When the flower is dry, brush on a small amount of peach petal dust at the base of the outer petals.

12. Finish your dahlia with a small amount of moss green petal dust, brushed onto the very center of the flower.

anemone

The anemone has a strong black center and delicate
white petals, giving it a naturally graphic appearance.
It's a great flower to add to a soft arrangement
to add a modern touch.

YOU WILL NEED

- Gumpaste, black
- 18-gauge green floral wire, 5in
  (12.5cm) in length
- Tylose or CMC glue
- Black outdoor upholstery-weight
  thread
- Green floral tape
- Scissors
- Plain gelatin powder

- Petal dust, black
- Paint brush
- Pencil
- AD-0 wafer paper
- Embossing wheel
- Eight pieces of 32-gauge white
  cloth-covered floral wire, 5in
  (12.5cm) in length
- Bowl of water

Depending on the brand of petal dust, you may need to add more to achieve a deep black color. However, be sure to not exceed a 50:50 ratio of gelatin to dust.

1. Create the anemone center by rolling a small ball of black gumpaste into a teardrop shape, with a diameter of about ⅜in (1cm), in the palm of your hand. Once you have the teardrop formed, dip approximately 1½in (4cm) of one end of the 18-gauge green cloth-covered wire into Tylose or CMC glue. Insert the glue-dipped end of the wire into the narrow end of the teardrop. Be sure to slide the wire well up into the thick part of the teardrop, but not so far that it pokes through the top. Smooth out the bottom end of the gumpaste, where it meets the wire, by twisting it between your fingertips to create a smooth and seamless transition from the teardrop to the wire.

2. Using your fingers, pinch and shape the top of your teardrop until it has a small, rounded peak and resembles a mushroom top. Set aside to dry for at least 24 hours.

3. Wrap the black outdoor upholstery thread around four of your fingers 150 times to create a dense loop of threads.

4. Remove the loop from your hand and loosely tack it together with a small amount of green floral tape. Place the floral tape about two-thirds of the way down the loop, creating a smaller loop at the bottom and a larger one at the top. Cut the bottom (smaller) loop open with scissors. Insert a dried gumpaste center through the middle of the top (larger) loop and pull through until it fits snugly. To secure the gumpaste center and hide the bottom threads, wrap them tightly with green floral tape. Once completed, use scissors to cut open the top threads and trim them down until they are level with the gumpaste center.

5. Combine two tablespoons of plain gelatin with one teaspoon of black petal dust and mix until the color is evenly distributed. Dampen the ends of your threads by brushing them with a wet paint brush. Once all thread tips are moistened, lightly dip them into the gelatin mixture. You will see the gelatin begin to slightly bloom when it attaches to the threads, creating the look of pollen.

6. Trace and cut out the anemone templates (see Templates) from a sheet of AD-0 white wafer paper. You will need four each of the small and large petals and eight back plate strips.

7. To vein your petals, place them one by one on top of a scrap piece of wafer paper and roll the embossing wheel over the entire surface, fanning outwards from the bottom center out past the top edge of the petal. Make multiple passes until the petal is completely covered in veins. Repeat this until all eight petals are veined.

8. Place the petals veined-side down and attach 32-gauge white cloth-covered wires to each by dipping 1–1½in (2.5–4cm) of one end of each wire into a bowl of water until it is just saturated. Immediately place the wet end of the wire onto the petal and sandwich it between the petal and a back plate strip. The wire should be placed ¼in (5mm) past the stem of each petal. Hold in place for a few

seconds so the water can soak into the back plate strip. Set aside to dry for approximately 20–30 minutes. Repeat the process for the remaining seven petals.

9. Once all the petals are dry, bend the base of the petal tab and wire by holding the petal, veined side up, between your fingers and gently pushing down on the the wire until it is at a 90-degree angle to the top of the petal. Repeat this process for each of the petals.

10. Starting with a small petal, place it at the base of the anemone center and secure it with green floral tape. Continue to place the remaining three small petals one at a time, slightly overlapping them each time you add a petal.

11. After all the small petals are attached, apply the four larger petals in the same sequence overlapping the seams of the smaller petals. Complete the flower by wrapping the floral tape down to the bottom, covering all the wires.

Poppy

These flowers come in a wide assortment of styles and colors to suit any palette. This particular poppy is an ornamental variety that is known for its vibrant center and soft petals.

YOU WILL NEED

- Gumpaste, pale green
- Craft knife
- 20-gauge green floral wire, 5in (12.5cm) in length
- Tylose or CMC glue
- Foam block
- White outdoor upholstery-weight thread
- Green floral tape
- Scissors
- Paint brush
- Petal dust, moss green and aubergine

- Paper towel
- AD-0 wafer paper
- Pencil
- Paper Potion, edible paper conditioner, in a spray container
- 2in (5cm) closed-cell styrofoam ball
- Four pieces of 32-gauge white cloth-covered floral wire, 5in (12.5cm) in length
- Bowl of water
- Clear Flo-Coat

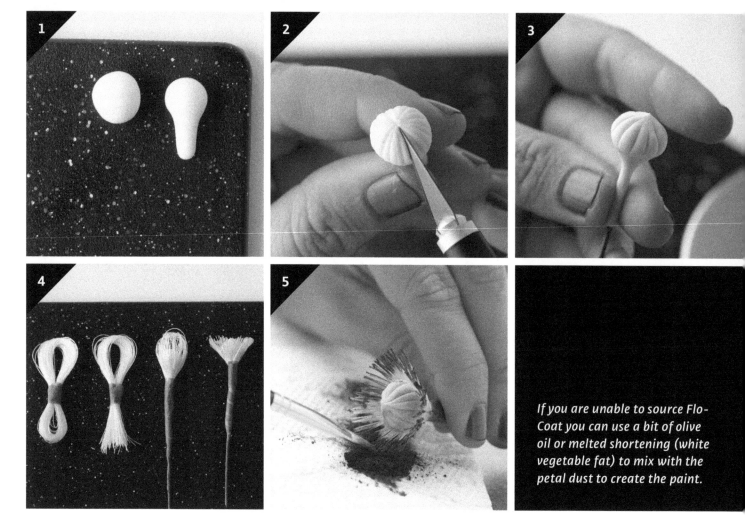

If you are unable to source Flo-Coat you can use a bit of olive oil or melted shortening (white vegetable fat) to mix with the petal dust to create the paint.

1. Take a small ball of pale green gumpaste and roll it in between the palm of your hand and finger to create a light-bulb shape.

2. Place the tip of a craft knife at the top center of the bulb and press down creating a straight indentation. Repeat multiple times, forming lines all the way around the bulb.

3. Next, dip the end of the 20-gauge green cloth-covered wire into Tylose or CMC glue and insert it into the narrow end of the bulb. Push the wire up until it reaches the bulb, but not so far that it pokes out the end. Then roll the narrow end between your fingers to thin it out and secure down the wire. Place the wire upright into a foam block to dry for 24 hours.

4. Create the flower stamens by wrapping the white outdoor upholstery-weight thread around four of your fingers about 75 times. Gently remove the thread and tack the loops together at the center with a small piece of green floral tape. Next, cut through the bottom loop with scissors and slide the gumpaste center through the top loops. Secure it by tightly wrapping green floral tape over the cut threads from the base of the bulb down to the end of the wire. Finally cut open the top looped threads and trim them down until they are the same height as the gumpaste center.

5. Working on a paper towel, apply a light dusting of moss green petal dust to the center to highlight the texture. Then apply a heavier coat of aubergine petal dust to the ends of the stamens, covering up most of the white thread. You may get a bit of the aubergine on the green center and that is ok. Set aside while you construct your petals.

6. Place the wafer paper on top of the poppy templates (see Templates) and trace over then with a pencil. Cut out four petals and four back plate strips.

7. Lay the four petals upside down (rough side up) and lightly spray with Paper Potion. Wait 60–90 seconds for the potion to soak in, then pick up one petal and place it smooth side up in the palm of your hand. Press the 2in (5cm) styrofoam ball firmly into the center of the petal while cupping your hand around them both. Release and set the petal aside. Use the same technique to shape the remaining three petals.

8. Next, dip the end of a 32-gauge white cloth-covered wire into a bowl of water. Using the styrofoam ball for stability, place the petal over it cupped side down and place the dampened wire over the back of the petal. Immediately place the back plate strip over it, sandwiching the wire between the petal and its backing. Press firmly to adhere all of the pieces together. Set aside to dry and repeat for the other three petals.

9. Once the petals are completely dry, mix a small amount of Flo-Coat and aubergine petal dust together. Paint the inside of each petal by brushing from the base up towards the top edge of the petal. Set aside to dry. Paint the remaining three petals.

10. Attach the dried petals to the center by first placing two of the petals, facing one another, around the center. Wrap green floral tape around them to secure them.

11. Then place the last two petals, facing one another and filling the gaps in between the previous petals. Wrap the floral tape around them to secure them, and continue winding it down the stem until it is fully covered.

Bougainvillea

Bougainvillea is a beautifully vibrant tropical flower that has gained recent popularity in the wedding industry due to its wide color range and natural, organic feel. Handfuls of these blooms can be made quickly and easily, and look stunning as a large arrangement on a cake, whether multi- or single-tiered.

YOU WILL NEED

- AD-4 wafer paper in bright pink
- Pencil
- Ruler
- Scissors
- Embossing wheel

- Three pieces of 32-gauge green cloth-covered floral wire, 4in (10cm) in length
- Bowl of water
- Green floral tape

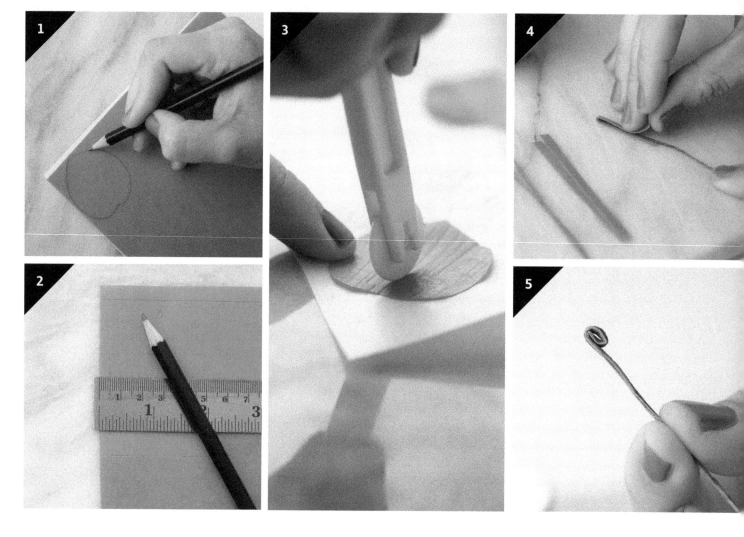

1. Place the wafer paper over the bougainvillea template (see Templates), trace and then cut out three petals.

2. Using a ruler and pencil, mark out and cut three strips of wafer paper that are ⅜in (1cm) wide and 3in (7.5cm) long. Set them aside while you prepare the petals.

3. First create a veined effect by placing the petals one by one atop a spare piece of wafer paper and rolling the embossing wheel over them repeatedly from the bottom of the petal out over the edges until each one is completely covered in veins.

4. Next, create the stamens of the flower by dipping a piece of 32-gauge green cloth-covered wire into a shallow bowl of water, submerging approximately 1½in (4cm) of the wire. Immediately place it halfway up one of the long strips of wafer paper that was cut out in step 2. Fold over the other half and press down firmly to sandwich and adhere the wire and the paper to one another.

5. Next, fold over the top of the stamen two times creating a small ball at the end.

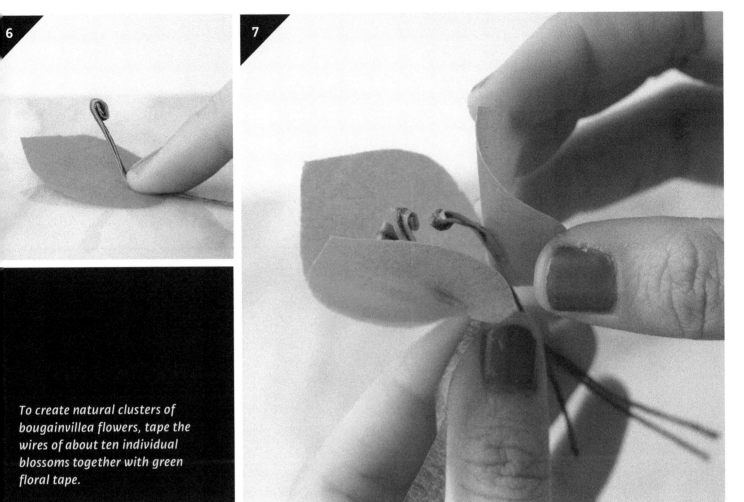

To create natural clusters of bougainvillea flowers, tape the wires of about ten individual blossoms together with green floral tape.

6. Then immediately place it onto the base of a petal that is veined side up, and press firmly to adhere them together. Set aside to dry and repeat steps 4–6 with the remaining two petals. Give the petals approximately 30 minutes to dry before moving on to step 7.

7. Once all three petals with the stamens attached are dry, they can be assembled using green floral tape. Starting with two petals, pull the tape around the wire stems twice to secure. Then place the third and final petal by holding the sides back slightly and sliding it into place. Once in place, wind the floral tape all the way down the wires to secure and hide them.

LEAVES:

Seeded Eucalyptus

While seeded eucalyptus can be a bit more time consuming to create than other greenery, it is well worth the extra effort for the impressive visual interest it provides to floral arrangements.

YOU WILL NEED

- Gumpaste, white
- 75 pieces of 32-gauge white cloth-covered floral wire, 4in (10cm) in length
- Tylose glue
- Two sheets of AD-0 wafer paper in soft green
- Shell and blade modeling tool
- Scissors
- Water
- Paint brushes

- 25 pieces of 32-gauge green cloth-covered floral wire, 4in (10cm) in length
- Paper towel
- Petal dust: foliage, chocolate and very dark chocolate
- White floral tape
- 22-gauge green or white cloth-covered floral wire, 12in (30cm) in length

1. Roll a tiny piece of white gumpaste between your thumb and forefinger to create a small teardrop shape that is about ⅓in (1cm) in diameter.

2. Dip the end of a 32-gauge white floral cloth-covered wire into Tylose glue and then immediately push the dipped end into the bulb end of the gumpaste teardrop. Set aside to dry. Repeat steps 1 and 2 until you have created 75 seeds. The seeds should be set aside to dry for 24 hours to ensure that they are securely attached.

3. While the seeds are drying, create the leaves by placing a single sheet of soft green wafer paper on top of the seeded eucalyptus template (see Templates) and trace over it using the blade side of the shell and blade tool.

Repeat until you have 25 leaves traced out on that one sheet of wafer paper. Now place this sheet on top of the second sheet of green wafer paper, rough sides together, and cut out each traced leaf using a pair of scissors.

4. Take a pair of the wafer paper leaves and brush a light coat of water on the rough side of one of the leaves. Immediately place a 32-gauge green cloth-covered wire on top of the damp leaf in the center approximately ¼in (5mm) down from the top of the leaf. Then press the second leaf on top of both bottom leaf and wire, making sure the green side is up. Press firmly over the whole leaf to make sure the two pieces adhere to one another, then set aside to dry. Note that the leaves may cup and curl naturally on their own while drying. Using this method, create a total of 25 two-sided leaves.

5. On a paper towel, mix the foliage petal dust with the chocolate petal dust, in a ratio of approximately three parts foliage to one part chocolate. In groups of six to seven seeds, gently brush the dust mixture on with an upward sweeping motion. Starting at the base of the petal (where the wire and seed meet), roll the seeds over and brush until the color is all the way around the seeds. Continue the same process until all 75 seeds are colored.

6. Once the seeds are all dusted, assemble them into small bunches of five seeds. Secure each bunch by tightly wrapping it together with white floral tape.

7. Next tape the leaves and seed bunches together by attaching them to the 22-gauge green or white cloth-covered floral wire with white floral tape. Attach one bunch of the seeds to the top of the wire and, winding the floral tape downwards, continue to add leaves and seeds randomly until about two thirds of the wire is covered. Cover the remaining exposed wire by continuing to wrap the floral tape all the way down to the end of the wire.

8. Complete your branch by dusting the stem with a small amount of foliage, chocolate and dark chocolate colored petal dust. As you apply the dust, mix the colors along the stem to give it a natural, mottled finish.

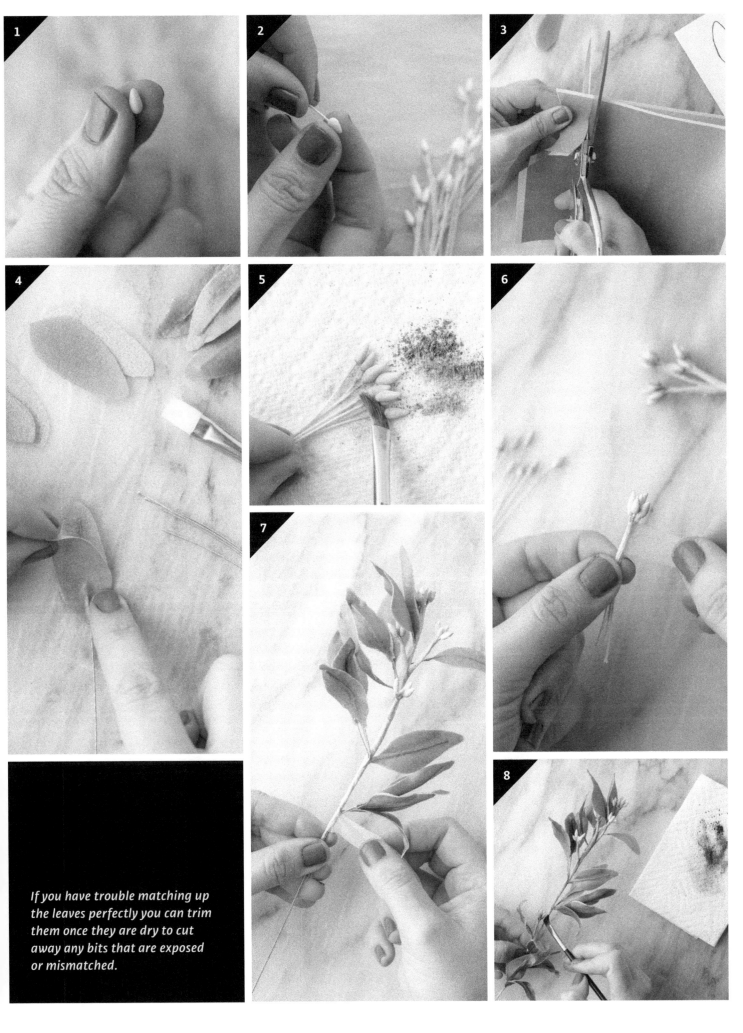

If you have trouble matching up the leaves perfectly you can trim them once they are dry to cut away any bits that are exposed or mismatched.

LEAVES:

Round Eucalyptus

Pale blue-green leaves with a soft brown stem, round eucalyptus is a beautiful foliage element to use when structure is needed to modernize an unrefined flower or loose floral arrangement. Its stem consists of a heavy gauge wire allowing you to easily shape and move it to the best position needed for your cake designs.

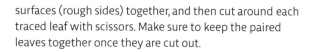

YOU WILL NEED

- Two sheets of AD-0 wafer paper in pale blue
- Gumpaste, white
- Tylose glue
- 22-gauge green cloth-covered floral wire, 12in (30cm) in length
- Shell and blade modeling tool
- Scissors

- Water
- Paint brushes
- 60 pieces of 32-gauge white cloth-covered floral wire, 3in (7.5cm) in length
- White floral tape
- Petal dust: chocolate, foliage and peach

1. Create a very small teardrop shape using white gumpaste, by rolling it between your thumb and forefinger.

2. Dip one end of the 22-gauge green cloth-covered floral wire into Tylose glue, and wipe away any excess glue – you do not want it dripping – then immediately insert the damp wire end into the bulb side of the gumpaste teardrop. Set aside to dry for approximately 12–24 hours.

3. Next take one sheet of the pale blue wafer paper and place it on top of the rounded eucalyptus leaf templates (see Templates). Trace around each leaf using the blade end of the shell and blade tool. You will need a total of 10 each of the mini and small sizes, 12 each of the medium and semi-medium sizes and 16 of the large leaves. Once all of the leaves are traced onto the wafer sheet, place that sheet on top of the second sheet with their reverse

surfaces (rough sides) together, and then cut around each traced leaf with scissors. Make sure to keep the paired leaves together once they are cut out.

4. Working on one leaf at a time, place one side of the paired leaf rough side up and apply a thin layer of water using a damp paint brush. Lay a 32-gauge white cloth-covered floral wire at the center of the damp leaf. Place the other (dry) half directly on top to sandwich and secure the wire between the two halves. Press firmly to help adhere the leaf together, and set aside to dry. Repeat this process for all of the pairs of cut leaves.

5. Once the wired leaves are dry, you can begin to assemble the eucalyptus with white floral tape. Starting with the smallest leaves, place one at the base of the gumpaste bulb. Wrap the floral tape around the wire of the leaf once and then place a matching sized petal directly opposite the previously placed one. Continue this process of adding the leaves to the branch in succession of sizing, from smallest to largest. Each time you add a pair of petals they should be placed directly opposite one another, but they do not need to be placed directly beneath the previous pair. Once all of the pairs are added to the branch, be sure to to wrap the tape all the way down to cover the remaining green branch wire.

6. To finish the eucalyptus branch, lightly dust over the white floral tape with a mix of petal dusts in foliage and chocolate. Also dust over the gumpaste teardrop at the tip with a bit of peach colored dust.

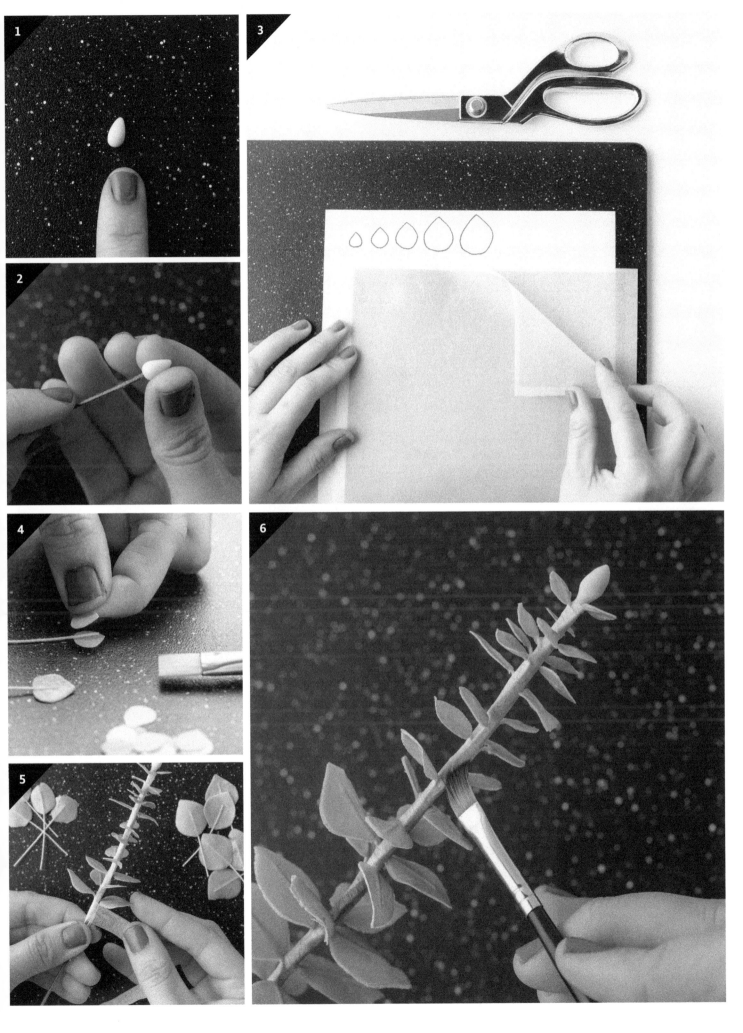

Citrus Leaf

Bright green and airy, the citrus leaf provides a pop of color and subtle movement that will liven up your cake design. The leaves can be made in quantity and stored for future use.

YOU WILL NEED

- AD-4 wafer paper in white
- Shell and blade modeling tool
- Scissors
- Vodka (or other clear high-alcohol-content liquid)
- Paint brush
- Gel color, lime green
- Two-sided silicone leaf veiner (see Suppliers)
- 32-gauge green cloth-covered floral wire, 5in (12.5cm) in length

1. Place the wafer paper sheet over the citrus leaf template (see Templates) and trace over it with the blade end of the shell and blade tool, leaving an indentation of the leaf on the wafer paper. Use a pair of scissors to cut the leaf out.

2. In a bowl, mix a small amount of the lime green gel color and vodka until you achieve a thin consistency.

3. Using a downward motion and starting at the top (the pointed end) of the leaf, paint both sides with a very small amount of the color mixture.

4. Next place the leaf directly into the bottom half of the leaf veiner. Press down firmly with the top half. Remove from the veiner and set aside to dry completely.

5. Cut a small piece of wafer paper approximately ⅛in (3mm) wide and 2½in (6.5cm) long. Brush on a very thin coat of the colored mixture over this strip. Wrap it around the 32-gauge green cloth-covered floral wire.

6. As soon as you have wrapped the wire with the strip, immediately place it on the back of the dried leaf, directly in the center. It should be placed so that the bottom of the wrapped part matches up with the bottom edge of the leaf.

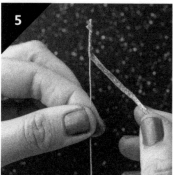

LEAVES:

Rose Leaf

Rose leaves are a beautiful go-to filler leaf. The deep emerald green color complements many design palettes and offers a natural element without weighing down the arrangement. The construction yields a very life-like and lightweight leaf that can be added to a multitude of flower combinations.

YOU WILL NEED

- Two sheets of AD-4 wafer paper in white
- Shell and blade modeling tool
- Scissors
- Vodka (or other clear high-alcohol-content liquid)
- Gel colors, forest green and black
- Paint brushes
- Two-sided silicone leaf veiner (see Suppliers)
- 32-gauge green cloth-covered floral wire, 4in (10cm) long

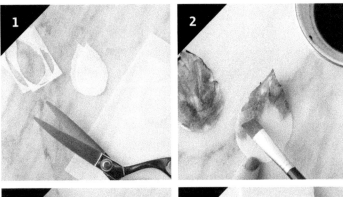

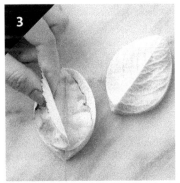

1. Place one piece of white wafer paper over the rose leaf template (see Templates), smooth side up, and trace over it using the blade side of the shell and blade modeling tool. Next, place the wafer paper on top of the second sheet so that their reverse surfaces (rough sides) are together, and the template is facing up. Cut the leaves out together using scissors.

2. Mix a small amount of forest green and black gel color in a small bowl, and then add small amounts of vodka to the mix until it becomes thin in consistency while still remaining a deep, dark green in color. Lightly paint over the smooth sides of the leaves, starting at the top (pointed) edges and working down towards the bottom, rounded part of the leaf.

3. Next, place one of the leaves colored side down onto one side of the leaf veiner. Then place a 32-gauge green cloth-covered wire at the center, extending it up to approximately ¼in (5mm) away from the top point of

the leaf. Place the second leaf colored side up over the wire, making sure to match it to the bottom leaf.

4. Press the top half of the veiner over the assembled leaf with heavy pressure. This will ensure that both halves of the leaf fuse together, and that the wire will stay in place between them. Remove the leaf from the veiner and set it aside to dry. The leaves will begin to take on different shapes as they dry. Repeat these steps to create as many leaves as are needed for your project.

LEAVES:

Fern

Light and airy fern branches bring a fun, almost magical influence to cake designs. Impressive for their scale, they are relatively easy to create and require only a couple branches at most to add a touch of wildness to any arrangement.

YOU WILL NEED

- Two sheets of AD-4 wafer paper in green
- Shell and blade modeling tool
- Scissors
- Water
- Paint brushes
- 14 pieces of 32-gauge green cloth-covered floral wire, 3½in (9cm) in length
- 22-gauge white cloth-covered floral wire, 14in (35.5cm) in length
- White floral tape
- Paper towel
- Petal dusts, forest green and black
- Cornstarch (cornflour)

1. Mark out one top leaf by placing one sheet of the wafer paper color-side up over the fern template (see Templates) and running the blade end of the shell and blade tool over it. The tool will leave an indentation. Then use the same method to trace out two each of the seven single-leaf templates for a total of 14 leaves. Place the wafer paper with the leaves marked on it back to back (rough sides touching) with the second sheet of paper. Then cut all of the leaves out using scissors. Make sure to keep the pairs of leaves together to make assembly easier.

2. Place one side of the top leaf color-side down, with the white rough side of the paper facing up. Brush on a very small amount of water over the entire leaf. Place the 32-gauge green cloth-covered floral wire in the center of the damp leaf and then carefully align and press the second leaf, color side up (rough side down), over the wire. Press firmly to secure the two sides of the leaf together. Set aside to dry. Repeat this technique with all 14 of the single leaves.

3. Once the leaves are dry, use a pair of scissors to cut small slits approximately every ⅛in (3mm) up the side of the leaf starting at the bottom and ending where the wire ends towards the top of the leaf. Mirror those slits on the other side of the leaf. Cut up to the center wire but be careful to not cut through it. Do this for all 14 leaves and the top leaf.

4. Shape the ends of each slit by clipping off the corners of each one of them. Do this for all 14 leaves and the top leaf.

5. Wrap white floral tape around the 22-gauge white cloth-covered floral wire at the base right below the bottom of the top leaf. Next, add the two smallest leaves opposite one another and secure them by wrapping the floral tape around their wires. Continue down the wire adding the pairs of leaves opposite one another, from smallest to largest, leaving approximately ½–¾in (1–2cm) of space between each pair. When all of the leaves are attached, wind the floral tape all the way down the rest of the wire, covering all of the exposed white cloth.

6. Pour approximately an eighth of a teaspoon of forest green petal dust onto a paper towel. Add a pinch of black petal dust to it and blend the colors together. Then add a bit of cornstarch (cornflour) until the color is a shade deeper than that of the leaves. Brush on the color over the white-taped branch.

1

2

3

If you don't have an edible printer (see Coloring & Printing), this is a good leaf to use the dry petal dust coloring method on. Dry dust the sheets with a light grayish green dust prior to tracing and cutting out the petals.

4

5

If you are creating multiple fern branches, you can make some of them with fewer fronds to create branches that are different sizes for a more natural look.

6

Decorations

Bows

Both dainty and playful, these wafer paper bows make the perfect addition to a multitude of projects. Their structured shape allows you to customize the look with any pattern, print, or color without compromising its modern quality, and can even be scaled larger or smaller for a twist on a design.

YOU WILL NEED

- AD-O wafer paper in color or pattern of choice
- Scissors
- Shell and blade modeling tool
- Water
- Paint brush

1. Place the wafer paper on top of the bow templates (see Templates) and trace over all three pieces using the shell and blade modeling tool to mark the outline of each, then cut them out with a pair of scissors.

2. Place the body of the bow, the largest of the three pieces, upside down (rough side up) and paint on a very light coat of water at the center.

3. Fold over each of the ends, one at a time, and secure them onto the damp center by pressing the end of the paint brush on top of the ends.

4. Next, lay the tail piece of the bow smooth side up and apply a very small amount of water at the center. Place the formed bow body on top of the tail piece and again secure by pressing them together with the end of the paint brush.

5. Finally, wrap the small center piece around the middle of the bow, smooth side up, and secure it at the back with a small amount of water. Set the bow aside to dry.

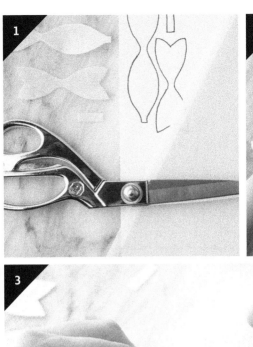

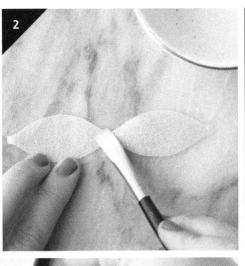

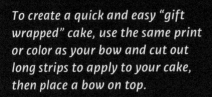

To create a quick and easy "gift wrapped" cake, use the same print or color as your bow and cut out long strips to apply to your cake, then place a bow on top.

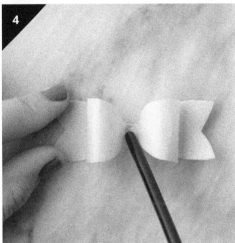

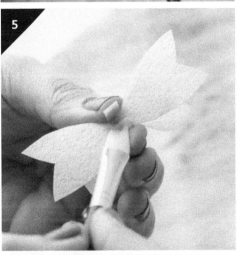

These bows can be used on gumpaste figures to add realistic looking bow ties or hair bows.

Wreath

This playful element can be used in numerous ways: try it on a holiday-themed or wedding cake surrounded by flowers.

YOU WILL NEED

- 22-gauge white cloth-covered floral wire, 12in (30cm) in length
- AD-0 wafer paper in color or pattern of choice
- White floral tape l
- Shell and blade modeling too
- Scissors
- Water
- Paint brush

1. Shape the 22-gauge wire into a 4in (10cm) diameter circle. This can be done by hand or by shaping it around any round object. Secure the ends together by wrapping them with white floral wire. Set aside.

2. Cut out two strips of wafer paper that measure approximately ¼in (5mm) wide by 11in (28cm) long. Brush on a small amount of water along the rough side of one of the strips. Immediately begin to wrap one wafer strip, damp side down, around the circle to cover up the wire. You may need to add more water as you go. Continue on with the second piece until the entire circle is covered in the wafer paper strips. Set aside.

3. Place a sheet of wafer paper over the wreath template (see Templates) and trace over it with the blade side of the shell and blade modeling tool. Use this method to mark out approximately 45 leaves. You can change to a different patterned paper for variety, and you may need more or fewer leaves depending on how full you want your wreath to be. Cut them out with scissors.

4. Next, give your leaves some depth by gently folding and bending them randomly.

5. Attach the leaves to the wafer-paper-covered circle with a small amount of water. Place them randomly around the circumference of the circle until it is completely covered.

Various gumpaste elements, such as berries, can be added to the wreath for added interest and accent.

Confetti

The quickest way to create a party cake is to add a little – or a lot! – of confetti. This edible wafer paper version can easily be customized to fit all party themes, simply by changing the color and shape of the pieces.

YOU WILL NEED

- AD-0 wafer paper in bright pink, light pink, dark green and metallic gold
- Paper punches, hexagon and small circle
- Hole punch
- Mini hole punch
- Scissors
- Paper Potion, edible paper conditioner, in a spray container
- Paint brush

1. Using the various paper punches and hole punches, cut out shapes from each of the wafer paper colors until you have created the desired amount of confetti.

2. Holding a full page of wafer paper lengthwise, cut narrow strips in varying widths.

3. Once the desired amount of strips are cut, place them on your work surface rough side up and lightly mist them with a fine coat of Paper Potion. Allow the potion to soak in for 60–90 seconds.

4. When the strips are pliable, wrap them gently around the handle of a paint brush to create curls. Gently remove them from the brush and set aside to dry.

To speed up the process, you may layer two sheets of wafer paper together while punching.

TOPPERS:

Garland

This garland adds a touch of bohemian spirit and is easy to customize with different shapes.

YOU WILL NEED

- AD-0 wafer paper in green
- Paper punches, single-leaf and multi-leaf
- Six pieces of 32-gauge green cloth-covered floral wire, 6in (15cm) long
- Water
- Paint brush
- Foam block
- AD-4 wafer paper in metallic gold
- Shell and blade modeling tool
- Scissors
- One piece of 18-gauge green cloth-covered floral wire, 11in (28cm) long

1. Punch out about 60 multi-leaf and 90 single-leaf pieces from green wafer paper. You may need more or fewer based on how the branches are constructed.

2. Place about ten multi-leaf and 15 single-leaf pieces, randomly overlapping, along half the length of one of the 6in (15cm) 32-gauge wires. Adhere the leaves with a little water. Hang over the side of foam block to dry for around 12 hours. Create a total of six branches.

3. Prepare your monogram topper by placing the gold wafer paper under the number template (see Templates), then trace over it with the blade of the shell and blade tool. This will leave an indentation on the gold paper that you can follow to cut out with scissors.

4. Create the armature by bending the 11in (28cm) long 18-gauge green wire into an "L" that is 8in (20cm) on its long side and 3in (7.5cm) on its short side.

5. Attach the number to the short side of the wire "L" by folding the tab on the top over, and using a small amount of water to tack it down.

6. Wrap the branches around the "L", starting on the short side, and covering 3in (7.5cm) of the long side.

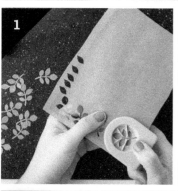

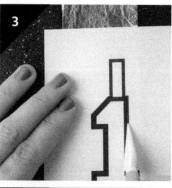
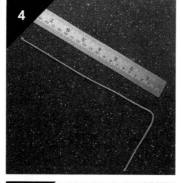
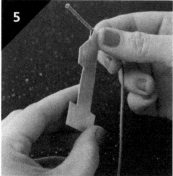

TOPPERS:

Swan

Make this sweet swan in minutes and add a touch of whimsy to any cake design.

YOU WILL NEED

- Wafer cardstock
- Shell and blade modeling tool
- Scissors
- Paint brushes
- Edible paint, black and peach
- Water
- Flat sandwich picks

1. Place the wafer cardstock over the swan template (see Templates) and trace over the template with the pointed end of your shell and blade tool. Use scissors to cut out two of the swan body template pieces and two each of the three wing pieces, and six spacers.

2. Place the swan bodies face-to-face (to help with accuracy while painting) and paint the beak with peach edible paint. Next, outline the tops of the beaks with black paint. Set aside to dry for about 30 minutes.

3. Once the faces are dry, flip over the swans and brush a very light coating of water over one of the bodies.

4. Place a sandwich pick on top of the dampened swan body and, making sure the swans line up correctly, place the second (dry) swan body on top. Press firmly to make sure the layers adhere to one another.

5. Fold the spacers in half, then take the largest part of the wing and adhere one side of a spacer to it with a little water. The folded end of the spacer should point towards the bottom corner of the wing. Next, attach the medium wing piece to the spacer with a dab of water and press firmly to adhere. Repeat to add the second spacer and smallest wing piece. The spacers should be sandwiched so they cannot be seen, and all the pointed ends should align at the bottom corner of the wing. Repeat to make the second wing.

6. With a little water, attach the wings to each side of the swan. Place them just in front of the sandwich pick so that they match up on both sides.

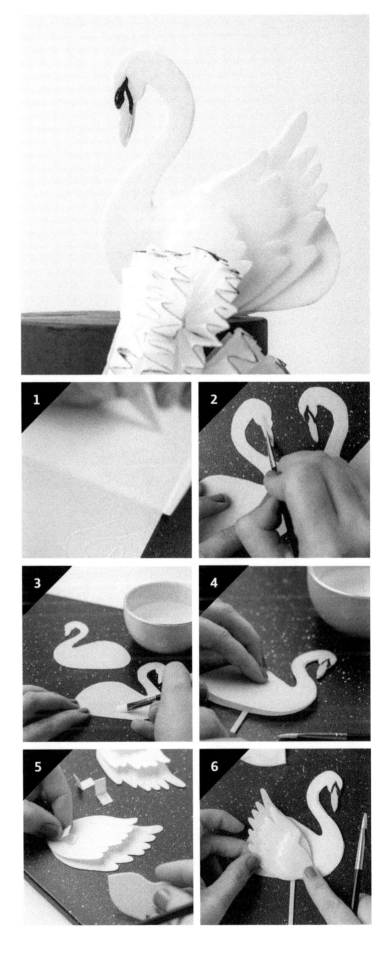

TOPPERS:

Geometric

This topper is a fun twist on traditional origami. It looks precarious, but the wafer paper is so light that it is actually quite secure.

YOU WILL NEED

- AD-0 wafer paper in white, black and light pink
- Ruler
- Shell and blade modeling tool
- Scissors
- Piping gel
- Paint brush
- Bamboo skewer, 4½in (11.5cm) long
- Foam block

1. Place the wafer paper face down (rough side up) on top of each of the templates (see Templates) and, using the ruler as a guide, trace over each of the lines with the pointed end of your shell and blade tool. It is important to keep the lines straight. Do this for all three shapes using all three colors of wafer paper.

2. Carefully cut out each shape. Make sure to cut only the outline, where the solid lines are on the template.

3. Fold over the small tabs on the shapes, using the dotted lines from the template as a guide. To assemble, place a small amount of piping gel on the color (smooth) side of the tabs and fold over the sides of the shape.

4. Finish by tucking the last tab into the side of the shape. Repeat steps 3 and 4 for the remaining two shapes. Set them aside to dry for 12 hours.

5. To assemble the geometric topper, place the skewer into the foam block with 1¾in (4.5cm) sticking out from the foam. Place the pink diamond on top of the skewer first, then use piping gel to secure the other two shapes on top of the diamond. Allow the topper to set and dry for at least 24 hours.

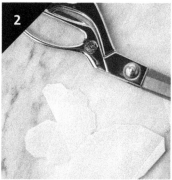

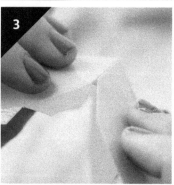

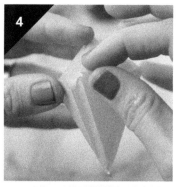

Extra thick piping gel works best for stacking the shapes. To create thick gel, leave a small amount in an open container overnight to dry out a bit.

TOPPERS:

Cactus

This quick and easy topper is quirky but very on trend. It is simple to assemble, making it a great option for all celebratory events.

YOU WILL NEED

- Wafer cardstock
- Shell and blade modeling tool
- Ruler
- Scissors
- Paint brush
- Edible paint, black and white
- Water
- Craft fringe scissors
- AD-0 wafer paper in bright pink

1. Place the wafer cardstock over the cactus templates (see Templates) and trace over them with the shell and blade tool. Use a ruler to ensure the straight lines are traced perfectly. Then cut out the pieces of your cactus.

2. After the pieces are cut out, paint the front of the cactus with black edible paint. Allow it to dry and then paint small white marks to create the cactus thorns. Allow to dry and then do the same on the reverse side.

3. Once both sides are dry, slide the armless piece over the piece with arms making sure it fits snugly and flush. The cactus should be able to stand on its own. If it doesn't, trim down the slits until it will. Once it can stand up, put a small amount of water where the slits meet the side of the cactus to secure them together. Set aside to dry.

4. Using craft fringe scissors, cut a fringe into a strip of bright pink wafer paper that is approximately 1in (2.5cm) long by ½in (1cm) wide. Once the fringe is cut, add a small amount of water at the base (below the fringe) and then roll it up to create a small "flower". Repeat this step to create a second "flower".

5. Stick the flowers on top and on one arm of the cactus with a small amount of water.

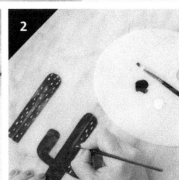

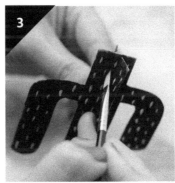

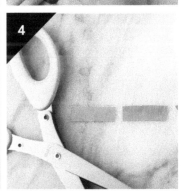

If you need to attach this topper more firmly, a flat sandwich pick can be added to the reverse side of the cactus and then inserted into the cake.

TEXTURES:

Leather

Leather is an unusual and dramatic look on a cake, but achievable due to the versatile nature of wafer paper.

YOU WILL NEED

- Fondant-covered cake tier
- Fabric tape measure
- Ruler
- AD-0 wafer paper, colored or printed black
- Scissors
- Paper Potion, edible paper conditioner, in a spray container
- Petal dust, black
- Large fluffy brush
- Water
- Paint brush

1. Measure the height and circumference of your cake tier with your fabric tape measure and ruler. Measure and cut the wafer paper sheets to the correct height and length. Multiple sheets may be needed to cover the whole of the tier.

2. Working with one sheet at a time lay them upside down (rough side facing up), and lightly spray the entire surface with Paper Potion.

3. Allow the potion to permeate the sheet for 10–20 seconds and then pick it up and crumple the wafer paper sheet with your hands.

4. Gently open the paper and flatten it out on your work surface to release some of the large creases but still leave the texture intact. Repeat steps 2–4 for all of your cut pieces of wafer paper.

5. Next, dip a large fluffy brush in black petal dust and brush it over the surface of the paper in large circular motions to highlight the texture and give it a more matte, "worn leather" look. Repeat with all the sheets.

6. To apply the sheets to the cake, brush a thin coat of water all over the sides of the cake tier. Once the cake sides are covered in water, gently press the wafer paper leather sheets onto the cake using a little more water to attach the seams together where the pieces meet up.

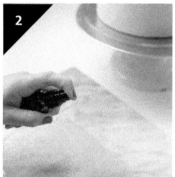

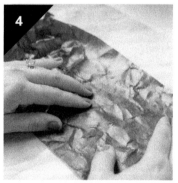

TEXTURES:

Metallic

Edible gold leaf is one of the most decadent and enduring favorites in the world of cake decorating. It can be a little on the expensive side, as it is pure 24-carat gold, but layering it onto wafer paper provides stability to the delicate leaves and gives you the choice of using it in sparse or abundant quantities. Once the metallic paper is made, it can be cut with scissors or paper punches to create countless designs, to allow you to add fully-edible gold accents to your cake creations.

YOU WILL NEED

- AD-0 wafer paper
- Piping gel
- Paint brush
- Edible gold leaf transfer sheets
- Large fluffy brush

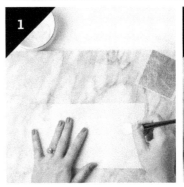

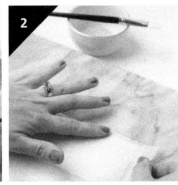

1. Brush to cover the smooth front side of the sheet of wafer paper with a thin coat of piping gel.

2. Carefully place a transfer sheet, gold side down, on top of the piping-gel-covered paper. Buff over the reverse side of the transfer paper with your fingers to ensure that the gold adheres the piping gel.

3. Gently pull back the transfer sheet, leaving the gold behind on the wafer paper. If, while pulling the sheet back, some of the gold is removed with it, lay the sheet back down and rub again with your fingers, then remove the clean transfer sheet.

4. Continue to repeat step 3 until the wafer paper is covered with gold leaf, then gently run a large fluffy brush over the surface to remove any loose leafing.

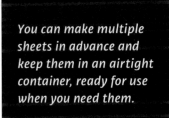

You can make multiple sheets in advance and keep them in an airtight container, ready for use when you need them.

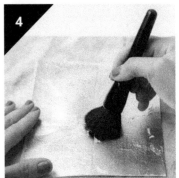

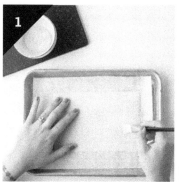

TEXTURES:

Glitter

Edible glitter is an exciting element to use in cake decorating, and can transform any design into an instant party! While fun, it can also be quite messy to work with, but applying it to wafer paper will give you more control over any glitter fallout. And since you can cut, punch, and shape wafer paper into numerous sizes and shapes, you'll find endless creative ways to work with this medium. Full sheets can even be used to cover entire cake tiers.

YOU WILL NEED

- AD-O wafer paper
- Parchment paper (baking parchment), larger than your sheet of wafer paper
- Baking sheet (tray) or similar
- Piping gel
- Paint brush
- Edible glitter – gold disco dust
- Foam brush

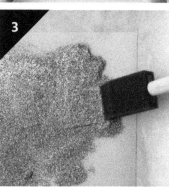

Use glitter to highlight accent items on sculpted gumpaste figures or as small elements within a cake design.

1. Place a piece of parchment paper (baking parchment) inside a baking tray and then place your wafer paper on top of that. The parchment and baking sheet (tray) will help control any excess glitter. Brush piping gel over the entire front (smooth) side of the wafer paper.

2. Carefully pour the glitter from the container over the surface of the piping-gel-covered wafer paper.

3. Using a foam brush, lightly pull the glitter across the page until all areas are covered.

4. Lastly, pick up the wafer paper sheet and let the excess glitter fall onto the parchment paper. Set aside the glitter-covered wafer paper to dry for approximately 24 hours. Then use the parchment paper to pour the excess glitter back into the container.

TEXTURES:

Lace

This is a great way to add texture to your designs. It's a modern spin on the classic piped lacework that has long been a staple in the cake industry, and a simple way to contemporize your designs.

YOU WILL NEED

- Fondant-covered cake tier
- Fabric tape measure
- AD-4 wafer paper
- Scissors
- All-over-the-page paper punch (see Suppliers)
- Water
- Paint brush

1. With a fabric tape measure, find the circumference and height of your cake tier. Add ⅓in (1cm) to your measured circumference, to allow for application to the cake.

2. Measure out and cut the wafer paper to those measurements. If you need to use more than one sheet of wafer paper to wrap the cake tier, overlap them by ¼in (5mm) and apply a small amount of water between the overlapped sheets to secure them to one another.

3. Next, start to create the lace effect with the paper punch by lining it up in one corner of the wafer paper. Using the punch's guidelines, cut out the lace pattern from the whole sheet of paper.

4. Once the entire paper is punched, wrap it around your cake tier. Brush on a small amount of water to the overlapped sections of paper and press the edges to secure them to one another. There is no need to attach the paper lace to the cake itself. Not attaching the paper directly to the cake will help combat any changes in the paper due to refrigeration or humidity that could result in it wrinkling.

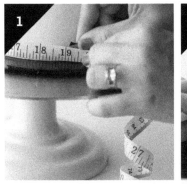

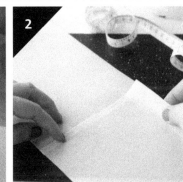

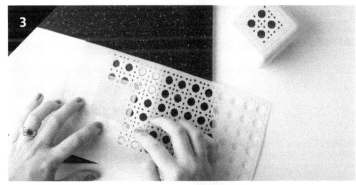

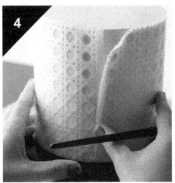

You can use this technique to create small borders or accents for your cake by cutting your lace sheets into different height pieces.

Decoupage

Decoupage is the art of decorating objects by gluing paper cut-outs to them. Wafer paper is the perfect medium to help translate this timeless technique into an edible version.

YOU WILL NEED

- AD-0 wafer paper in five or six mixed prints and/or colors
- Scissors
- Piping gel
- Paint brush
- White fondant-covered cake tier

1. With a pair of scissors, cut the wafer paper into varying sizes and shapes. In this case, we are creating a geometric look so the shapes will reflect that. But this technique can be used with any shape, size, or color variation to suit your design.

2. Once all of your wafer paper is cut, brush a thin layer of piping gel directly on the fondant, starting at the bottom edge and working up towards the middle of the cake tier. It's best to apply the gel in small sections at a time so that it does not dry out before you are able to attach the wafer paper shapes.

3. Starting at the bottom edge, place your first piece of wafer paper. If your shape does not already have a straight edge that can be matched to the bottom edge of the cake, be sure to trim it before applying it.

4. Next, start placing other shapes in varying colors, prints and sizes around the first piece you placed, fitting the shapes as closely together as possible so the fondant is no longer visible. Continue this process around the entire tier.

5. To create depth and texture, randomly layer a few more pieces over the already placed shapes. To do this, apply a small amount of piping gel directly to the reverse of the shape.

6. Then apply the shape directly to the cake, overlapping the previous shapes.

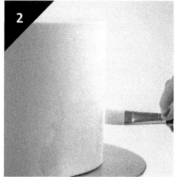
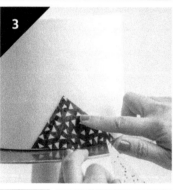
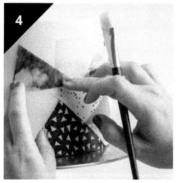
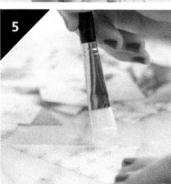
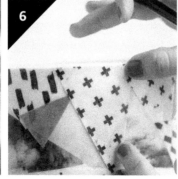

TEXTURES:

Ruffles

Light and airy, ruffles offer a unique texture.

YOU WILL NEED

- AD-0 wafer paper
- Piping gel
- Paint brush
- Fondant-covered cake tier

1. Begin by tearing multiple sheets of wafer paper lengthwise, going with the grain. This will give you more control over your torn edges. Each strip should be roughly ¾–1in (2–2.5cm) in width. However, they will vary so don't focus too much on getting them all exactly the same. The amount of strips that you need will depend on the size of your cake tier. As a general reference, two sheets are needed to cover a round tier that is 5in (12.5cm) in diameter and 6in (15cm) in height.

2. Set aside the pieces that have one straight edge and one ruffled – those will be used for the final row. Next, apply a liberal coating of piping gel to your cake tier, covering the cake sides completely. If you are working with a very large tier of cake, 12in (30cm) or larger, you can work in sections to prevent the piping gel from drying out before you get to adding the ruffles.

3. Start by adding one strip to the top of the cake. It should sit slightly higher than the edge of the tier. Continue around using as many strips as needed to encompass the entire circumference. Slightly overlap the previously placed ruffle with each new strip.

4. Place the next row of ruffled strips lower than the first row, and slightly overlapping the seams of the row above it, ensuring that the fondant is completely covered. Press the ruffles into the piping gel to secure them. Repeat this method while making each new row slightly further down the cake, until you have roughly one "row" of fondant still visible.

5. Use the strips with the one straight edge, which you set aside earlier, for the bottom row. The straight edge of the strips should fit flush against the base of the cake.

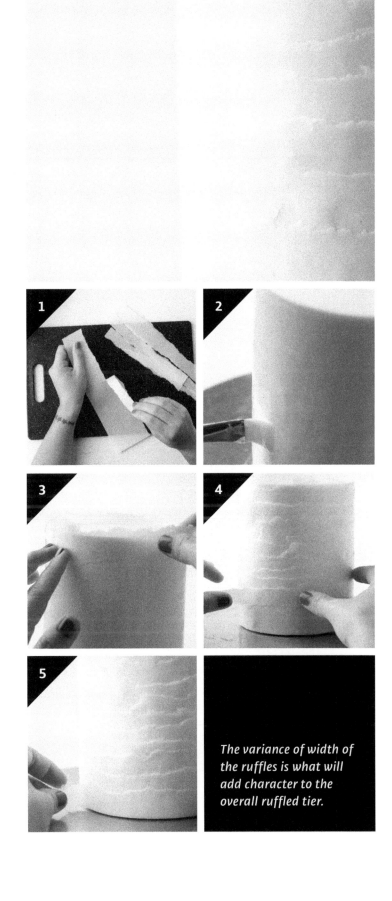

The variance of width of the ruffles is what will add character to the overall ruffled tier.

Cakes

Subtly Avant Garde

Adding black abstract paint and gold studs gives this cake a modern edge and a more contemporary vibe. However, adding the romantic pastel ranunculus with their abundant petals and delicate green centers effortlessly softens the design, producing a beautiful, well-rounded cake suitable for numerous occasions.

YOU WILL NEED

- Thin paint brush
- Edible paint, black
- Wax paper, at least the height of each cake tier and 6in (15cm) wide
- Three stacked cake tiers, covered with white fondant: 4in (10cm) diameter by 6in (15cm) high, 6in (15cm) diameter by 6in (15cm) high, and 6in (15cm) diameter by 8in (20cm) high
- Gumpaste, white
- Silicone pyramid mold

- Small rolling pin
- Craft knife
- Water
- Gold highlighter dust
- Lemon extract
- Flat-bristled paint brush, ¼in (5mm)
- 1½in (4cm) styrofoam ball
- White candy melts
- Wafer paper flowers (see Flowers): 12–15 ranunculus

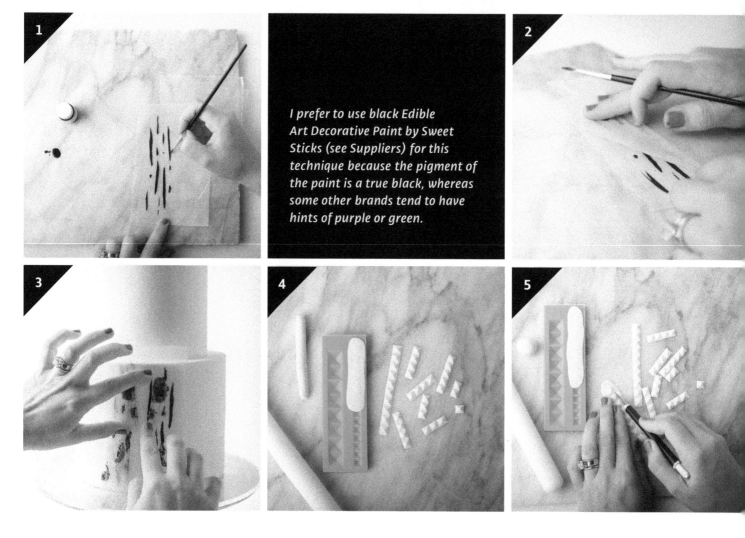

I prefer to use black Edible Art Decorative Paint by Sweet Sticks (see Suppliers) for this technique because the pigment of the paint is a true black, whereas some other brands tend to have hints of purple or green.

1. Using a thin paint brush and black edible paint, paint multiple lines and dots of differing sizes on half of your wax paper rectangle. Your painted lines and dots should be thick and opaque.

2. Once the lines and dots are painted, fold over the wax paper lengthwise, sandwiching the paint between the layers. Gently rub the wax paper to spread the paint.

3. Unfold the wax paper and press the painted side onto the first cake tier, lightly rubbing the paper on the unpainted side to transfer the paint. Gently peel back the wax paper and discard. Repeat steps 1–3 for the other two tiers of the cake.

4. Create the stud details by rolling a small amount of white gumpaste into a rope-like shape slightly larger than the pyramid mold cavity. Press the gumpaste rope into the mold using a small rolling pin.

5. Unmold and clean up any excess edges with a craft knife. Also using the craft knife, cut the molded row of studs into varying lengths. Set aside to dry.

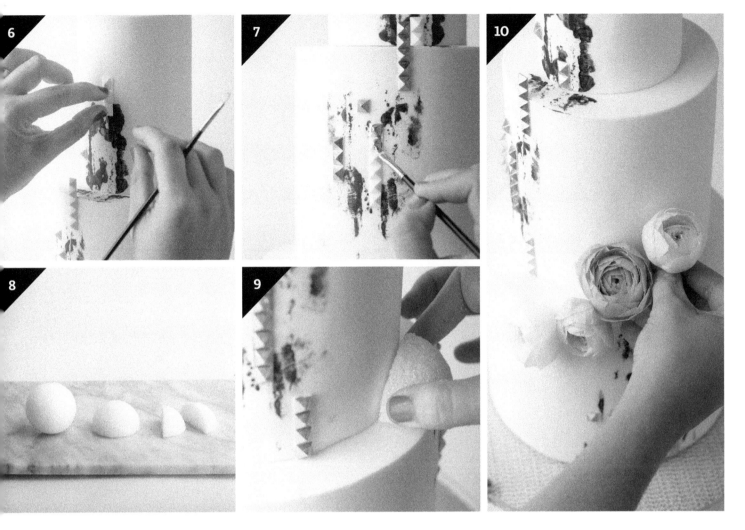

6. Once dry, attach the studs to the cake by applying a small amount of water to the back and pressing them, at random, over the painted areas of the cake.

7. Mix a small amount of gold highlighter dust with lemon extract until you have a loose paste-like consistency. Using a ¼in (5mm) flat-bristled paint brush, carefully paint all of the studs gold.

8. To create the flower arrangements, cut a 1½in (4cm) styrofoam ball in half; reserve one half for the top arrangement and cut the remaining half in half again.

9. Using melted white candy melts, cover the flat sides of the exposed, quartered styrofoam and place on the ledge between the bottom and middle tier. Using more melted chocolate, cover the flat side of the halved styrofoam and place on the top of the top tier.

10. Place the ranunculus' wire stems into the styrofoam, closely positioning each flower to create organic-looking, natural arrangements, until the styrofoam pieces on the top and on side of the cake are no longer exposed.

Gilded & Gray

The simple modern aesthetic of this gray-and-gold tiered-cake is heightened by a contrastingly over-sized arrangement. By mixing the understated with the exuberant, the overall design is an unexpected and fresh spin on more traditional designs.

YOU WILL NEED

- 12in (30cm) acrylic cake board
- Three stacked cake tiers, covered with dark gray fondant: 4in (10cm) diameter by 6in (15cm) high, 6in (15cm) diameter by 6in (15cm) high, and 8in (20cm) diameter by 6in (15cm) high
- Small bowl
- Gold highlighter dust
- Lemon extract
- Paint brush
- Styrofoam cone, with 2in (5cm) diameter base, 5cm (12.5cm) tall

- White candy melts
- Needle-nose pliers
- Wire cutters
- Wafer paper flowers (see Flowers):
  2 David Austin roses
  3 standard roses
  5 ranunculus
  3 anemone
  3–5 buds of ranunculus or roses
  2 fern branches
  1 seeded eucalyptus branch

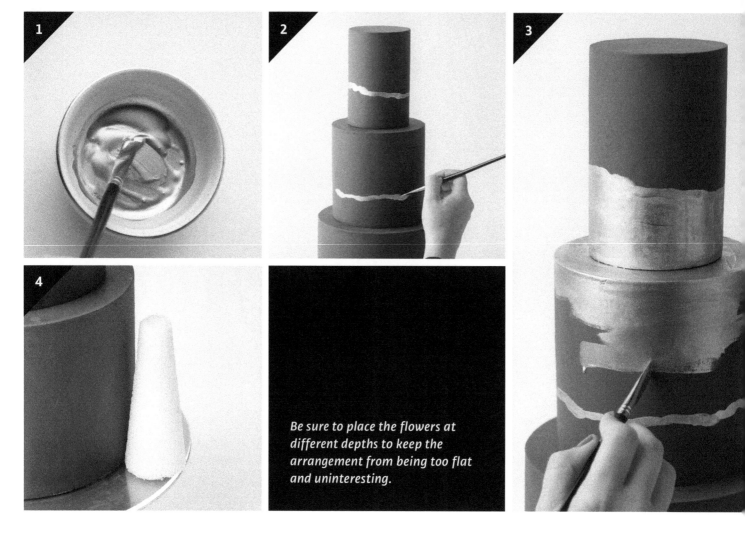

Be sure to place the flowers at different depths to keep the arrangement from being too flat and uninteresting.

1. In a small bowl, mix the gold highlighter dust and lemon extract to a medium consistency. It is important that the mixture is reasonably thick so that when it is painted on the cake it will not create any drips, but offer consistent opaque coverage.

2. Paint a rough, uneven line around the circumference of the top tier, approximately two-thirds of the way down from the top. Do the same around the second tier.

3. Paint between the two lines with the gold mixture until it is a solid gold band around the cake tier.

4. Next, apply the styrofoam cone to the acrylic board using heated white candy melts. Position the cone so it is slightly to the right of your cake. Allow it to dry for approximately 10 minutes.

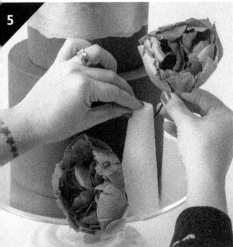

5. Once the cone is firmly secured to the board, begin to arrange the wafer flowers by starting with the largest blooms first, in this case the David Austin roses. Place them in prominent positions to complement your cake, one at the bottom of the arrangement and one at the top.

6. Start to fill in the gap between them with the other full-sized flowers. A pair of needle-nose pliers are helpful during this process to place the flowers where your fingers can't reach. You may also need to use wire cutters to trim down the wires of the flowers so that they sit properly into the styrofoam.

7. At this point your styrofoam should be mostly covered. If there are any small spaces or foam visible, fill in those spots with small buds.

8. To finish your design place one fern branch at the bottom of the arrangement and one at the top. And finally place the seeded eucalyptus branch at the top next to the fern. You can bend the branches as needed to give movement to the arrangement.

Elegant Minimalism

With a contemporary color palette of black and white, this cake design makes for a bold statement based simply upon contrast. Monochromatic accents help to highlight the structured qualities of the gold hexagon wreath and greenery, and allow the softness of a single large-scale dahlia to take center stage.

YOU WILL NEED

- Three stacked cake tiers: 4in (10cm) diameter by 6in (15cm) high covered in white fondant, 6in (15cm) diameter by 6in (15cm) high covered in black fondant, and 8in (20cm) diameter by 6in (15cm) high covered in black fondant
- Gumpaste, white and black
- Extruder tool
- Cardboard cut into an 8in (20cm) hexagon template
- Rolling pin, small and large
- Craft knife
- Ruler
- Clear ruler
- Water
- Paint brushes
- Gold highlighter dust
- Lemon extract
- Wafer paper flowers (see Flowers): 1 dahlia 4 round eucalyptus branches
- Green floral tape
- Piping gel
- Nine pieces of 22-gauge green cloth-covered floral wire, (12.5cm) in length
- White candy melts

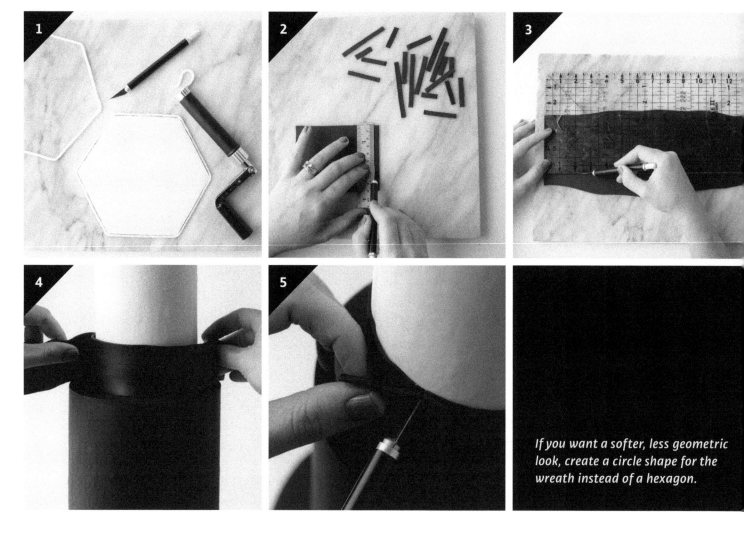

If you want a softer, less geometric look, create a circle shape for the wreath instead of a hexagon.

1. Place white gumpaste into the extruder tool with a ¼in (5mm) round disc attached to the end. Squeeze out a piece of gumpaste that is 22in (55cm) long. Place it around the outer edge of the cardboard hexagon template to shape it, and allow to dry for approximately 24 hours or until it's completely dried through.

2. Roll out some black gumpaste with a small rolling pin until it is roughly ¼in (5mm) thick. Cut the gumpaste down into multiple strips that are ¼in (5mm) wide and a variety of lengths between 2in (5cm) to 4in (10cm). Set them aside while you work on step 3.

3. With a large rolling pin, roll out black fondant to approximately ¹⁄₁₆in (2mm) thick and at least 2in (5cm) wide by 14in (35.5cm) long. Using a clear ruler, cut the fondant into a strip that is 2in (5cm) wide and 14in (35.5cm) long.

4. Brush a small amount of water along the bottom 2in (5cm) of the top tier. Place the fondant strip all the way around the base of the top tier, using the dampened border to adhere the fondant strip to the cake tier.

5. Trim down the excess fondant at the back of the cake with a craft knife to create a flush and smooth seam.

6. Attach the small strips of black gumpaste randomly, and at varying heights, along the front of all three cake tiers using a small amount of water.

7. Mix a small amount of gold highlighter dust with lemon extract to a medium-thick consistency. Paint the completely dry gumpaste hexagon with the gold paint. Let it dry while you work on step 8.

8. Place three eucalyptus branches together, with a fourth one pointing the opposite way. Secure the branches together with green floral tape.

9. Fold the pieces of 22-gauge wire into small "U" shapes. Use five of them to carefully attach and secure the gold hexagon to the top edge of the bottom tier of the cake.

10. Bend the eucalyptus branch to mimic the shape of the bottom of the gold hexagon. Attach it to the cake using the remaining four "U" shapes. To finish the design, place a small amount of heated white candy melts on the reverse of the dahlia and press it into the open spot between the eucalyptus branches. Hold it in place until the candy melts have hardened and the dahlia stays secure on its own.

Graceful Simplicity

This playful and delicate concept of tutus and swans is made contemporary and mature with the chosen color palette of black and rose gold. The addition of the hexagon separator tiers also lends a more sophisticated look.

YOU WILL NEED

- Two round cake tiers covered in black fondant: 4in (10cm) diameter by 6in (15cm) high, and 7in (18cm) diameter by 6in (15cm) high
- Two hexagon dummy cake tiers covered in white fondant: (13cm) across by 2in (5cm) high, and 8in (20cm) across by 2in (5cm) high

- Edible paint, rose gold and black
- Paint brushes
- Two sheets of AD-0 wafer paper in white
- One sheet of wafer cardstock
- Water
- Piping gel
- Swan topper (see Decorations)

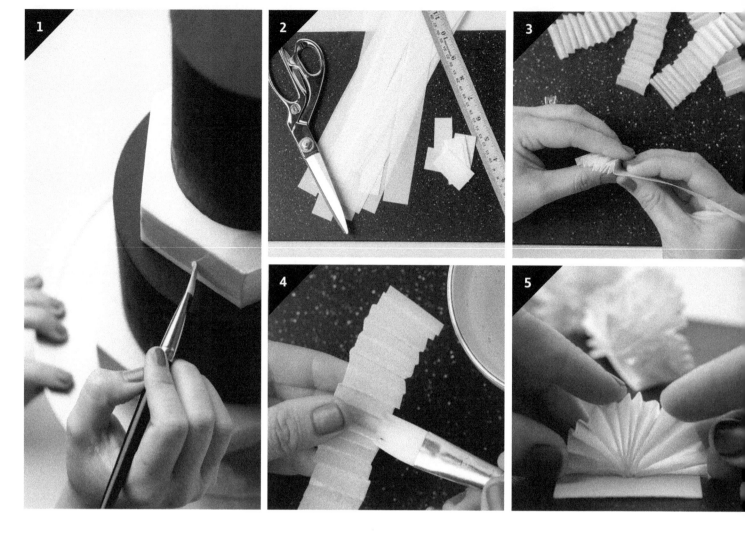

1. Stack the cake tiers in the order shown, then paint the hexagon tiers all over with the rose gold edible paint.

2. Next, cut down the AD-0 wafer paper into 27 strips that measure 1in (2.5cm) wide and 11in (28cm) long. Then cut nine pieces of the wafer cardstock into small rectangles that measure 1in (2.5cm) wide by 2in (5cm) long.

3. Now take each 11in (28cm) long strip and fold it like an accordion. Each fold should be approximately ¼in (5mm) wide. Fold all 27 pieces.

4. Brush on a very light coat of water along the entirety of one side of the accordion-folded paper.

5. Squeeze the accordion-folded paper at the base to create a fan. Brush a small amount of water on one of the wafer cardstock rectangles and press the fan down on top of it. Create two more fans by following steps 3 and 4 again. Then place each of them on the same wafer cardstock rectangle covering the majority (if not all) of the rectangle. Repeat steps 3–5 to create a total of nine assembled ruffles.

If you have trouble attaching your ruffles with piping gel, you can use melted white chocolate instead.

6. After all of the ruffles are assembled, attach them to the cake with a small amount of piping gel. Place a cluster of four, cascading down the right side of the top tier, and the remaining five ruffles cascading down the 7in (18cm) black fondant-covered tier.

7. Next, paint all the ruffle edges with a light coat of black edible paint to highlight the accordion folds.

8. Finish off the cake design by placing the swan topper behind the top ruffles.

Cactus & Confetti

The combination of cactus and confetti may be a bit unexpected but it creates a fun and festive cake that anyone would be happy to receive. And you can easily mix up the color palette to fit your next fiesta.

YOU WILL NEED

- Two stacked cake tiers covered in white fondant: 4in (10cm) diameter by 6in (15cm) high, and 6in (15cm) diameter by 6in (15cm) high
- One sheet of AD-0 wafer paper in white
- Scissors

- Piping gel
- Paint brush
- Small tray
- Wafer paper confetti (see Decorations)
- Three cactus toppers in varying sizes (see Decorations)

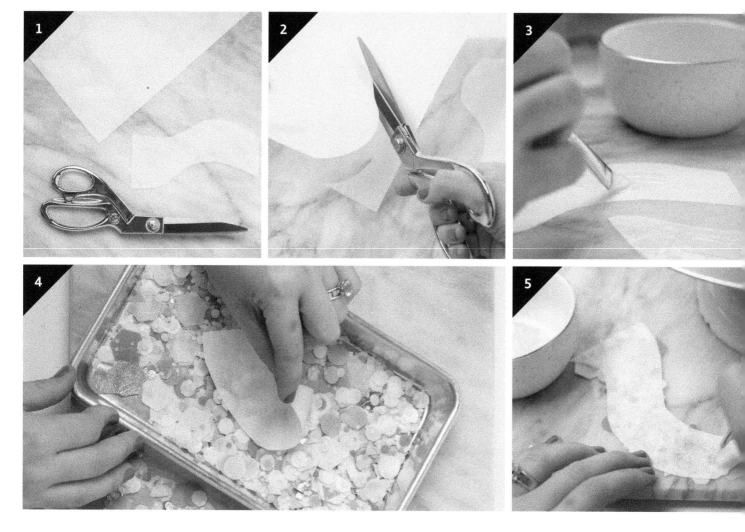

1. With a pair of scissors cut a loose "S" shape from the sheet of wafer paper. The "S" shape should be the same height as your cake tier, in this case 6in (15cm) tall, and roughly 3–4in (7.5–10cm) wide.

2. Next, cut a loose "C" shape from the remaining wafer paper that is approximately 3–4in (7.5–10cm) tall and 3–4in (7.5–10cm) wide.

3. Place both the "S" and "C" shapes front side (smooth side) up on your work surface. Brush on a liberal amount of piping gel all over this surface of the shapes.

4. Fill a small tray with all of the flat pieces of wafer paper confetti. Then dip your "S" and "C" shapes, piping gel side down, into the confetti. Move the paper around and press down as needed to cover all of the surface area of the shapes with confetti. Extra pieces can be added by hand to cover up any exposed areas if need be.

5. Once the shapes are completely covered, brush on a thin coat of piping gel over the entire reverse side of the "S" shape.

6. Next, attach the "S" shape to the top tier by pressing it onto the cake.

7. Repeat steps 5 and 6 to apply the "C" shape to the bottom tier of the cake.

8. Using piping gel to attach them, place additional pieces of confetti along the edges of the shapes to provide a more natural look as well as to cover up the exposed wafer paper edges of the shapes.

9. Next, add the wafer paper curls from the confetti mix over the existing confetti on the cake, using a small amount of piping gel.

10. To finish the design, apply a liberal amount of piping gel to the bottom of the cactus toppers and place two on the top tier and one on the ledge between the tiers.

Contemporary Edge

This celebration cake embraces a number of edgy textures and shapes, and rounds out the contemporary style with a softened color palette. Mimicking the sharp lines and edges of shattered sugar crystals, wafer paper gems add a touch of playfulness to the design.

YOU WILL NEED

- Three stacked cake tiers: 4in (10cm) diameter by 6in (15cm) high and 6in (15cm) diameter by 6in (15cm) high, both covered in white fondant; and 8in (20cm) diameter by 6in (15cm) high covered with leather texture (see Decorations)
- Isomalt nibs (see Suppliers), black and clear
- Silicone tray mold

- Gel colors: white, pink and cream
- Sandwich pick (cocktail stick)
- Large zip-closure food bags
- Kitchen hammer (tenderizer)
- White candy melts
- Paint brush
- Piping gel
- Geometric topper (see Decorations)
- Geometric shapes (made from topper template)

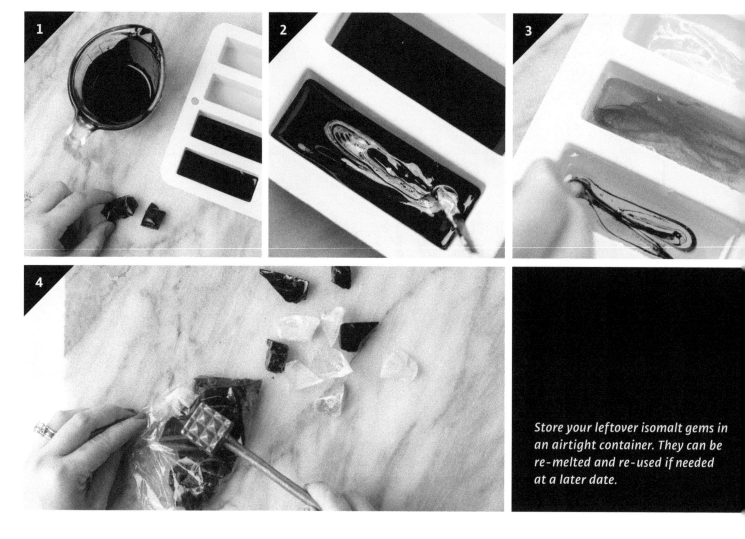

Store your leftover isomalt gems in an airtight container. They can be re-melted and re-used if needed at a later date.

1. Create black sugar crystals by melting down the black isomalt nibs, as per the manufacturer's instructions, and pouring into the silicone molds. Fill the molds approximately halfway.

2. Add a few drops of white gel color into the black isomalt in the molds and swirl around with a sandwich pick (cocktail stick), creating a marbled look. Do not mix too much, you don't want it to become a solid color. Set aside to harden and cool.

3. Repeat steps 1 and 2 with the clear nibs. Add the different gel colors to the clear isomalt to create various colored gems.

4. Once the molds are completely cooled and hardened, place each color into a large zip-closure food bag. Break the large molded pieces into small shards and gems by hitting them with the kitchen hammer (tenderizer). Pieces should be varied in size and shape. Repeat this step for all of the different colors you created.

5. Attach the sugar crystals to the left side of the top and middle tiers, and to the right side of the middle and leather-covered tiers, using a small amount of heated white candy melts. Make sure when you place the crystals to leave a few open spaces where you will add the wafer paper gems.

6. Using a small amount of piping gel, attach the wafer paper gems amongst the previously placed sugar crystals.

7. Finally, add the geometric topper on the far right edge of the top tier of the cake.

Tropical Textures

Inspired by the movement and textures of tropical foliage, this design embraces the wild feeling naturally associated with such greenery, but finds balance with a monochromatic simplicity. The bright-white color both softens and sharpens the untamed tropical arrangement, though this could also be easily used to contrast with the addition of a single accent color for a fun twist on the design.

YOU WILL NEED

- Two stacked cake tiers covered in white fondant: (12.5cm) diameter by 6in (15cm) high, and 7in (18cm) diameter by 6in (15cm) high
- Three sheets of wafer cardstock in white

- Shell and blade modeling tool
- Scissors
- Piping gel
- Paint brush
- White fondant
- Water

This design can quickly and easily be changed up by adding color. Paint the butterflies with edible paints to make them really pop against the white leaves.

1. Place a sheet of wafer cardstock over the tropical textures templates (see Templates), and trace around them with the blade side of the shell and blade modeling tool. Trace out seven butterflies, four palm fronds, three medium mostera leaves and two large mostera leaves.

2. Cut out all of the traced shapes with a pair of scissors.

3. Once all of the pieces are cut out, carefully fold back the wings of the butterflies to give them more shape and movement. Set aside.

4. Next, apply the leaves to the side of the cake using a small amount of piping gel to fix them in place. The first layer of the leaves should cascade down the entirety of the left side of the cake.

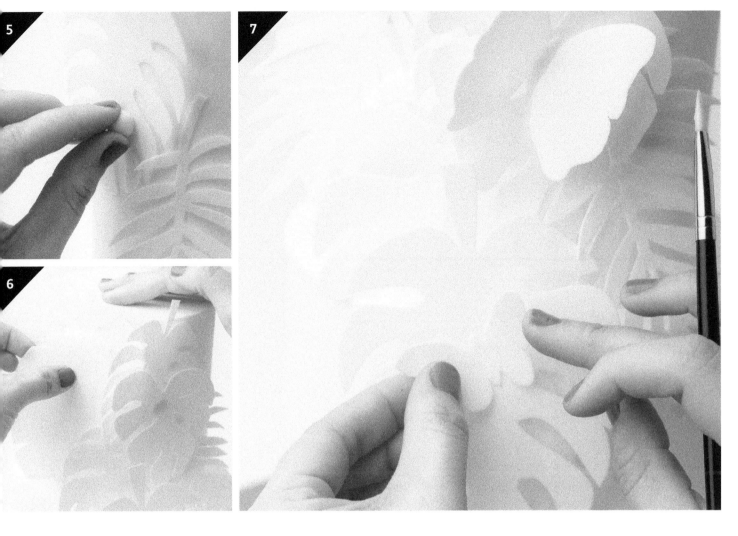

5. To attach the next layer of leaves, place a small ball of white fondant to the previously attached leaves. This will serve as a spacer, offering a small gap between the layers, and will help add interest to the draped arrangement. Use piping gel to attach the fondant ball.

6. Apply a thin coat of piping gel over the fondant ball, and then press the leaf onto it. Continue to follow steps 5 and 6 until all of the leaves are applied.

7. Once all of the leaves are attached, place the butterflies randomly around the leaves by brushing on a small amount of water to the reverse side of each butterfly and then pressing it onto the leaves.

Celestial Celebration

In a modern take on childhood lullabies, this design pulls
inspiration from some of the current astrological trends.
Easily adaptable to numerous celebrations, this design can be
used as a starting point to customize a unique, brilliant cake
for birthdays, anniversaries, baby showers, and more.

YOU WILL NEED

- Two cake tiers covered in white
  fondant: (12.5cm) diameter by
  6in (15cm) high, and 7in (18cm)
  diameter by 6in (15cm) high
- Three sheets of AD-0 wafer paper
  in deep rose
- 6 x 6in (15 x 15cm) metallic gold
  wafer paper (see Decorations)
- Various star paper punches

- Reference photo of constellation
  of choice
- Piping gel
- Gold highlighter dust
- Lemon extract
- Paint bushes
- Garland topper with metallic
  moon (see Decorations)

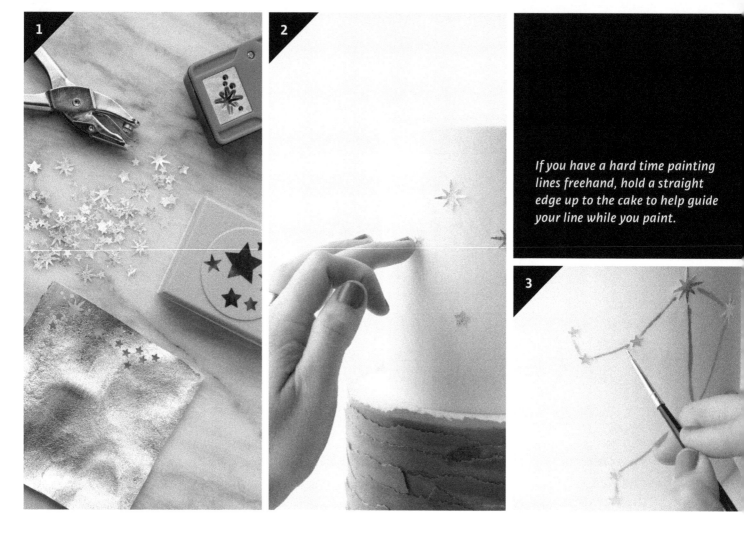

1. Prepare the 7in (18cm) cake by covering it in deep rose wafer paper ruffles (see Decorations). Next, stack your cake using your preferred method and set aside. Then punch out a large amount of variously shaped and sized stars from the metallic gold wafer paper using the paper punches.

2. Using your constellation reference picture, place stars on the top tier of cake to replicate their positioning. Use a small amount of piping gel to attach them.

3. Once the main stars of the constellation are placed, mix the gold highlighter dust with a small amount of lemon extract to create a paint that is of medium consistency. Use a small brush to draw in the constellation lines, connecting the stars and finishing the constellation's full shape.

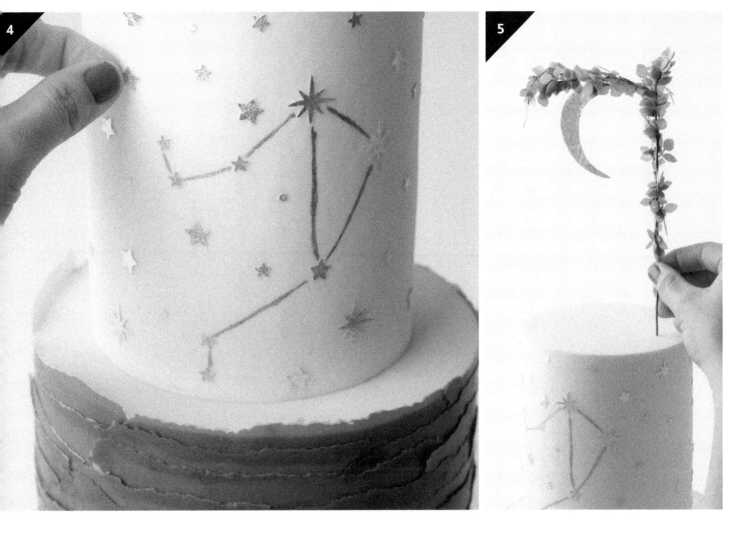

4. After the constellation is complete, attach the remaining punched out stars randomly around the entire top tier, and around the constellation, again using a small amount of piping gel to secure them. If you find it difficult to attach the small stars, use the end of a paint brush or a pair of tweezers to place and secure them.

5. Trace the moon template (see Templates) onto wafer paper, cut out and add to a garland topper (see Decorations). To finish the design, insert the garland and moon topper to the top tier. Be sure to place it close to the far right edge of your top tier so that the moon is approximately hanging at the center of the tier. And only push it down into the cake until the garland is touching the top of the cake and the bare wire is no longer visible.

Modestly Adorned

This design updates the classic details of a white, lace-inspired cake into a refined statement piece. The body of the cake is highlighted with a just-visible white-on-white texture, and is further accentuated by a bright pop of bougainvillea flowers and gold draping. The mix of textures and minimal color scheme results in a chic, yet romantic design and is sure to leave a lasting impression.

YOU WILL NEED

- Three cake tiers covered in white fondant: 4in (10cm) diameter by 6in (15cm) high, 6in (15cm) diameter by 6in (15cm) high, and 8in (20cm) diameter by 6in (15cm) high
- Lace texture wafer paper (see Decorations)
- Extruder tool
- White fondant
- Craft knife
- Paint brush
- Water
- Gold highlighter dust
- Lemon extract
- Bougainvillea, approximately 60 flowers (see Flowers)
- Green floral tape
- 2in (5cm) styrofoam ball, cut in half
- White candy melts
- Bamboo skewer

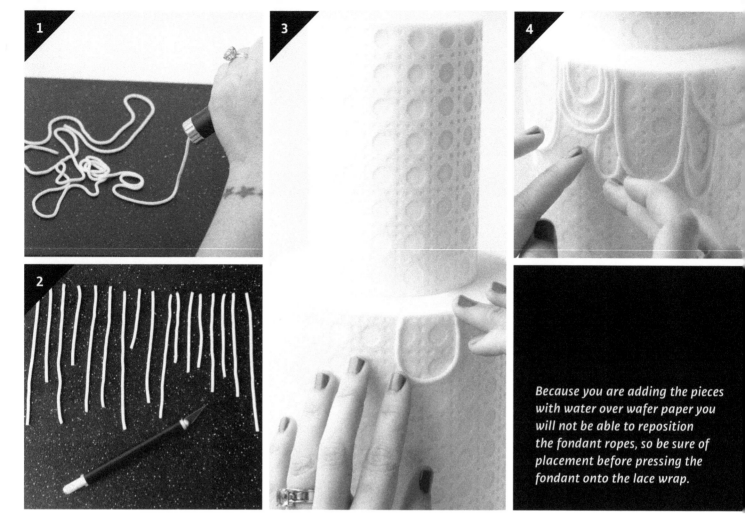

Because you are adding the pieces with water over wafer paper you will not be able to reposition the fondant ropes, so be sure of placement before pressing the fondant onto the lace wrap.

1. Wrap your cake tiers in lace texture wafer paper (see Decorations). Next stack your cakes using your preferred method, making sure any visible "seams" are aligned down the back of the cake. Once stacked, use the extruder tool with the ⅛in (3mm) hole disc attached to expel a long, white fondant rope.

2. Cut the fondant rope down into different length pieces, measuring as small as 3in (7.5cm) and as large as 6in (15cm), as well as various lengths in between.

3. Brush on a small amount of water to the back of one of the fondant ropes and apply it to the cake. Place one end of the piece on the top edge of the middle tier, allowing it to naturally drape, and then tack down the other end to the edge of the same tier with a small gap between them.

4. Continue on with the same technique to apply more fondant pieces. Due to the various lengths of the ropes, the drapes will vary in size, which is the look that you want to achieve. You can overlap multiple pieces, as well as drape shorter lengths in between existing drapes to create a more layered effect.

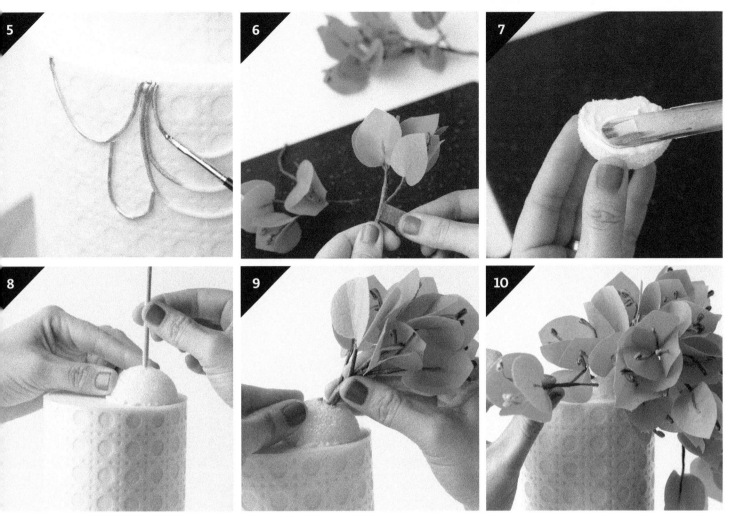

5. Next, mix the gold highlighter dust with a small amount of lemon extract until it is of medium consistency. With a small paint brush, carefully paint all of the draped fondant pieces with the gold paint.

6. Next, tape together roughly ten bougainvillea flowers with green floral tape, creating a small cluster. Make four separate clusters, leaving 20 individual blooms to use in step 10.

7. Cover the whole of the flat side of the styrofoam half-ball with heated white candy melts.

8. Place the styrofoam shape, chocolate side down, on to the top right edge of the top tier of cake. Secure it by inserting a bamboo skewer through the middle and down into the cake tier.

9. Insert the four bougainvillea clusters into the styrofoam, as close to one another as possible, but still covering up the majority of the ball.

10. Lastly, use a few individual blooms to fill in any gaps or cover any exposed styrofoam. Use the remaining individual blooms to create a small cascade, draping from the right side of the arrangement.

Modern Alignment

This progressive design is full of clean lines, attractive angles and an unexpected color palette. It is a bold pattern, but is softened with an elongated line of lush wafer paper blooms. While the impact is impressive, the technique for painting the shapes is quick and easy to achieve with a minimal amount of materials.

YOU WILL NEED

- Two stacked cake tiers: 5in (12.5cm) diameter by 6in (15cm) high, covered in peach fondant, and 7in (18cm) diameter by 6in (15cm) high, covered in white fondant
- Edible paints: peach, brown, gray and white
- Paint brushes
- Paint palette
- Painter's (masking) tape, narrow
- Gold highlighter dust
- Lemon extract

- White candy melts
- 3in (7.5cm) styrofoam ball, cut in half
- Needle-nose pliers
- Wire cutters
- Wafer paper flowers (see Flowers):
  1 peony
  3 garden roses
  4 ranunculus
  2 round eucalyptus branches

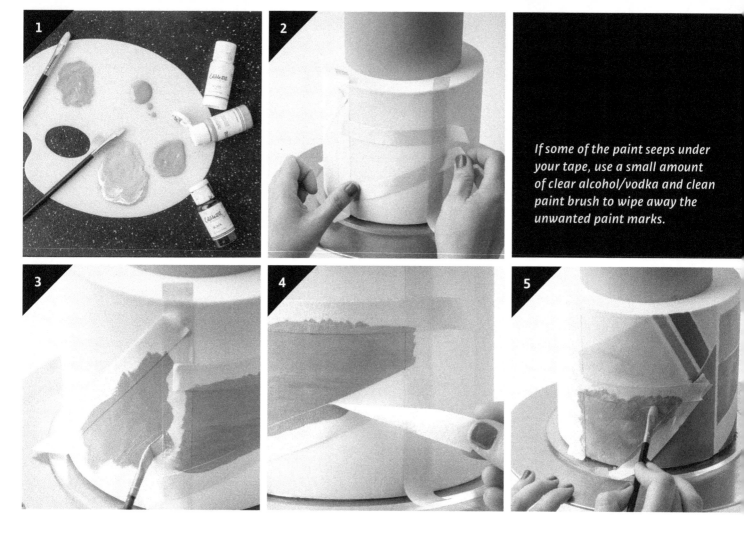

If some of the paint seeps under your tape, use a small amount of clear alcohol/vodka and clean paint brush to wipe away the unwanted paint marks.

1. Mix a small amount of the peach and brown edible paints together on the palette until you achieve the same shade as your top fondant-covered tier. Then squeeze out a small amount of gray into three separate spots on your paint palette. Add some white to the middle spot to create a shade of gray that is a little bit lighter than the full strength paint from the bottle. Then add a larger amount of white to the third spot to create a shade that is even lighter than the other two grays.

2. Next, apply narrow painter's (masking) tape to the white cake tier to mask off a few geometric shapes. Press firmly on the edge of the tape that is on the interior of the geometric shape to ensure that the paint will not seep underneath it.

3. Once a few of the shapes are masked off, paint them in with the different shades of paint. Choose the colors randomly, and leave some white as well. Leave the paint to dry thoroughly.

4. Remove the tape by pulling one end at an angle, away from the side of the cake.

5. Next, move on to different sections of the cake tier and repeat steps 2–4 until the fondant is covered in geometric shapes. This time, when applying the tape to the cake leave a gap that is approximately ¼in (5mm) between the existing painted shapes.

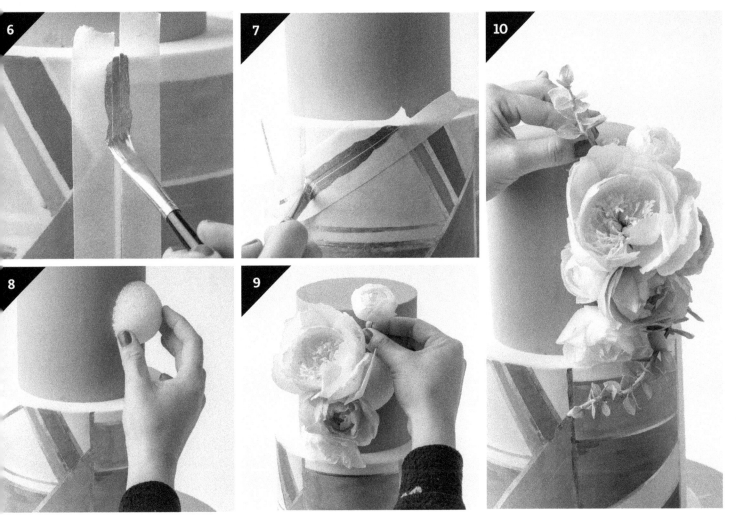

6. Once the tier is covered in painted shapes, allow it to dry completely. The timing for this will vary, but should take around 5–10 minutes. When the shapes are dry, begin to apply the painter's tape to line the ¼in (5mm) gaps. Paint those gaps in with a gold paint that can be created by mixing the gold highlighter dust with the lemon extract to a medium paste consistency.

7. Continue to repeat step 6 until all of the lines between the shapes are painted gold.

8. Using heated white candy melts, attach the styrofoam half-ball to the top tier of the cake. Place it just off to the right side, approximately halfway down the tier.

9. Apply the flowers in a vertical line starting with the peony first, and then adding in the other flowers to hide the styrofoam. Wire cutters can be used to cut down wires if needed. Also, needle-nose pliers can be used to help arrange flowers if necessary.

10. To finish the design, add the two round eucalyptus branches to the arrangement, one at the top and one at the bottom, bending them as needed to drape naturally over the cake.

Wild Beauty

Similar to an expressionist painting, this cake features abstract brushstrokes, but these are kept clean, tight and modern within sharp, linear boundaries. Merging these techniques, the design mimics a contained chaos that can be translated into any color palette and suits a multitude of celebratory occasions.

YOU WILL NEED

- Two stacked cake tiers covered in white fondant: 4in (10cm) diameter by 6in (15cm) high, and 6in (15cm) diameter by 6in (15cm) high
- Painter's (masking) tape, narrow
- Edible paints: pink, peach, white, gray, black and brown
- Paint brushes
- 3in (7.5cm) styrofoam ball, cut into quarters

- White candy melts
- Needle-nose pliers
- Wire cutters
- Wafer paper flowers (see Flowers):
  1 David Austin rose
  1 garden rose
  2 standard roses
  2 ranunculus
  1 seeded eucalyptus branch

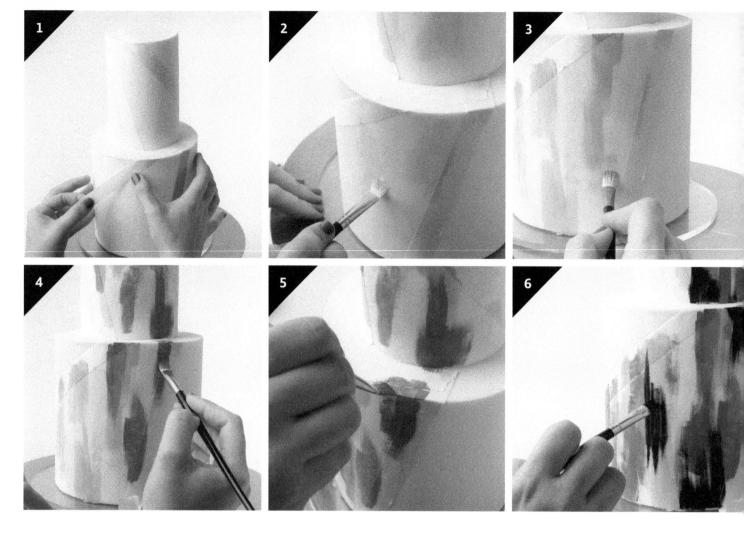

1. Use the narrow painter's (masking) tape to create two large angular shapes on the top and bottom tier of your cake. Press the edge of the tape that is on the interior of the shape down firmly with your fingers to help prevent the paints from seeping underneath.

2. Starting with the peach-colored edible paint, brush on small vertical paint striations, randomly placed in the spaces between the taped lines.

3. Using the same technique, create more of the same strokes with pink paint.

4. Next, repeat the process using the brown paint.

5. Add the gray paint in the same manner. At this point, approximately 80–90 per cent of the space between the tape should be filled with paint strokes.

6. Fill in the last few remaining exposed patches with the black paint.

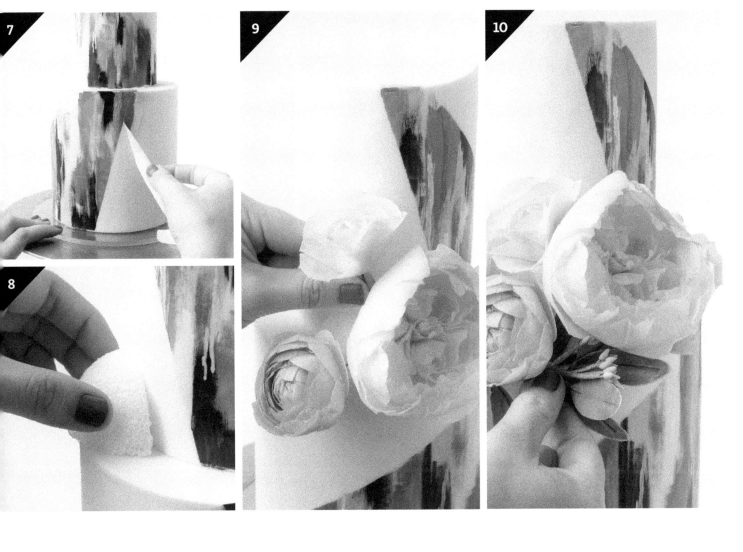

7. Finally, with a thin paint brush, add a few fine white lines randomly within the painted area to create some interest and to break up the look of all of the thicker striations. Once the painting is complete, remove the tape by pulling it gently at an angle, away from the side of the cake.

8. Using heated white candy melts, attach the quarter styrofoam ball to the left side of the cake between the two tiers. Allow it to dry for approximately 2–3 minutes.

9. Insert the flowers into the styrofoam, starting with the large David Austin rose towards the front of the cake, then adding the other flowers around the sides towards the back. The flowers should be arranged snugly around the side of the cake. Wire cutters can be used to cut down wires if needed. Also, needle-nose pliers can be used to help arrange flowers if necessary.

10. Lastly, add the seeded eucalyptus branch by inserting the wire end into the rear of the styrofoam and then bend it forward tucking it up underneath the flowers.

Modern & Marbled

This design embraces various distinctive design elements and combines them to produce one extrovertly modern cake. The sharp hexagon shapes are subdued by the organic marbled fondant, while the pinwheels with the gold studded centers offer a bit of quirky edginess.

YOU WILL NEED

- Three round cake tiers covered in white fondant: 4in (10cm) diameter by 6in (15cm) high, 6in (15cm) diameter by 6in (15cm) high, and 8in (20cm) diameter by 6in (15cm) high
- Hexagon dummy cake tiers, 10in (25cm) across by 2in (5cm) high
- Shortening (white vegetable fat)
- 1lb (450g) white fondant
- Black gel color
- Sandwich pick (cocktail stick)

- Large rolling pin
- Plastic wrap (cling film)
- White candy melts
- Hexagon cookie cutter
- Water
- Paint brushes
- Gold highlighter dust
- Lemon extract
- Six wafer paper pinwheels (see Flowers), in varying sizes and black and white prints

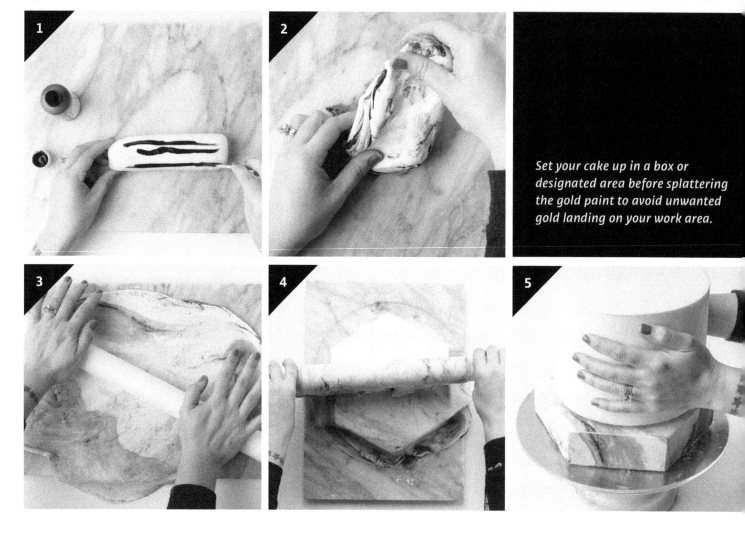

Set your cake up in a box or designated area before splattering the gold paint to avoid unwanted gold landing on your work area.

1. Prepare your hexagon dummy tier by rubbing a thin layer of shortening (white vegetable fat) over the surface. Then roll approximately 1lb (450g) of white fondant into a log. Using a sandwich pick (cocktail stick) spread black gel color in lines over the top of the log.

2. Carefully fold the log over onto itself, and begin to knead the fondant gently until the color starts to incorporate into it. Stop kneading before the color is completely mixed in, you want it to look marbled.

3. Roll the kneaded fondant out with a large rolling pin. It should be at least 14in (35.5cm) in diameter and ⅛in (3mm) in thickness when you have finished rolling it out.

4. Pick up the rolled fondant with your rolling pin and place on top of the shortening-covered hexagon dummy. Smooth down the sides of the fondant and remove the excess at the base of the tier. Do not knead the excess fondant back together, but rather reserve it for step 6 by setting it aside and covering it with plastic wrap (cling film) to prevent it from drying out too quickly.

5. Spread a small amount of heated white candy melts on top of the hexagon tier and stack the 8in (20cm) cake tier on top. Stack the rest of the tiers on top of that base using your preferred method of stacking cakes.

6. Using the reserved marbled fondant, roll the scrap sheets out to roughly 1⁄16 in (2mm) thick. Then cut out approximately 55 hexagons using the hexagon cookie cutter. Set them aside, and cover loosely with plastic wrap (cling film) to prevent them from drying out too quickly.

7. Starting at the bottom of the 6in (15cm) tier, apply the hexagon shapes, using a small amount of water. Place the first two or three rows tightly together like tiles. Once those rows are positioned, place a few hexagons randomly above the rows.

8. After all of the hexagons are placed, mix a small amount of gold highlighter dust and lemon extract in a bowl. The mixture should be of thin to medium consistency. Dip a paint brush into the mixture and immediately fling the brush towards the front of the cake creating a loose splatter effect, focusing mostly on the tier covered in hexagons. Repeat this process until the cake is splattered to your satisfaction.

9. Lastly, apply the pinwheels in a cascade down the front of the cake using melted candy melts as "glue". Hold each pinwheel briefly in place until it stays without sliding.

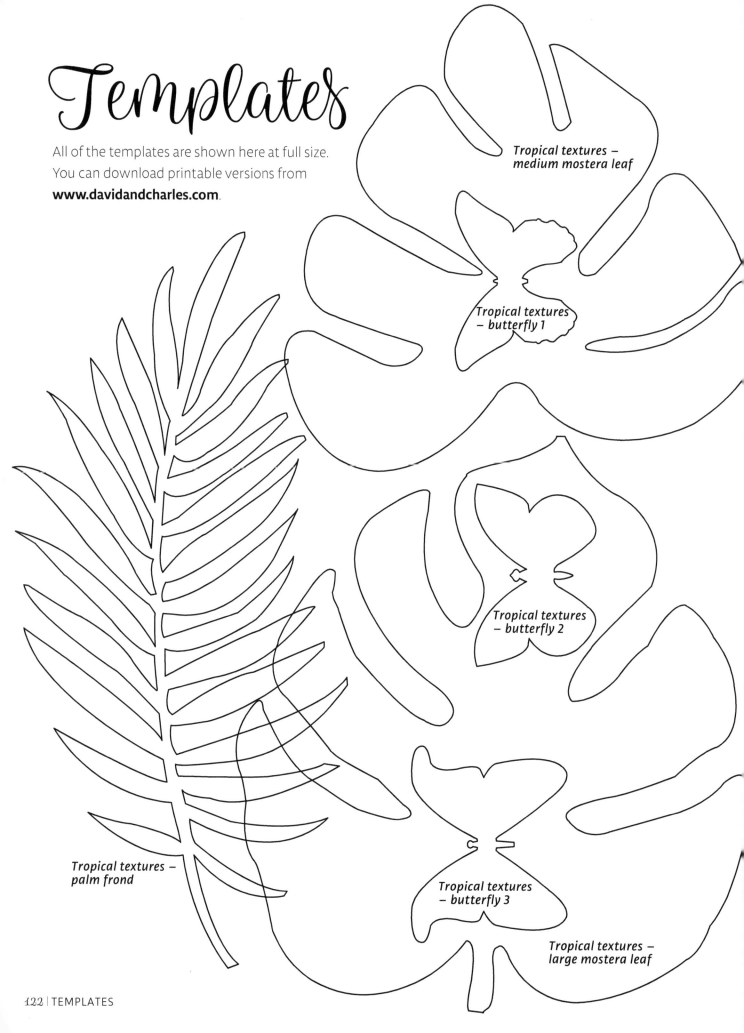

Templates

All of the templates are shown here at full size.
You can download printable versions from
www.davidandcharles.com.

Tropical textures –
medium mostera leaf

Tropical textures
– butterfly 1

Tropical textures
– butterfly 2

Tropical textures –
palm frond

Tropical textures
– butterfly 3

Tropical textures –
large mostera leaf

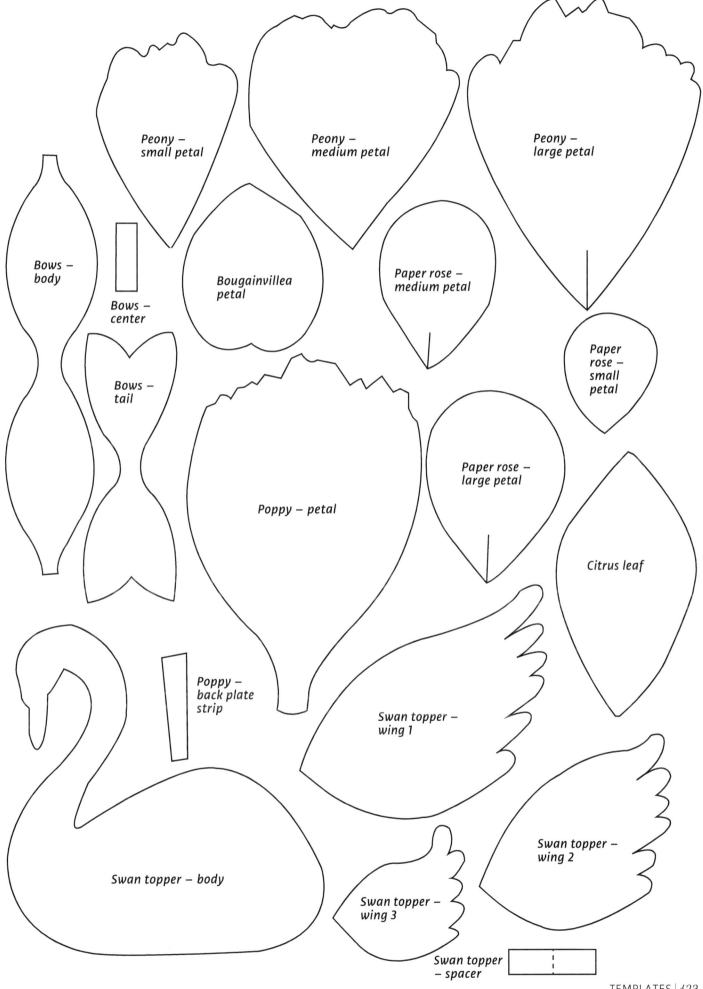

Peony – small petal

Peony – medium petal

Peony – large petal

Bows – body

Bows – center

Bougainvillea petal

Paper rose – medium petal

Paper rose – small petal

Bows – tail

Poppy – petal

Paper rose – large petal

Citrus leaf

Poppy – back plate strip

Swan topper – wing 1

Swan topper – wing 2

Swan topper – body

Swan topper – wing 3

Swan topper – spacer

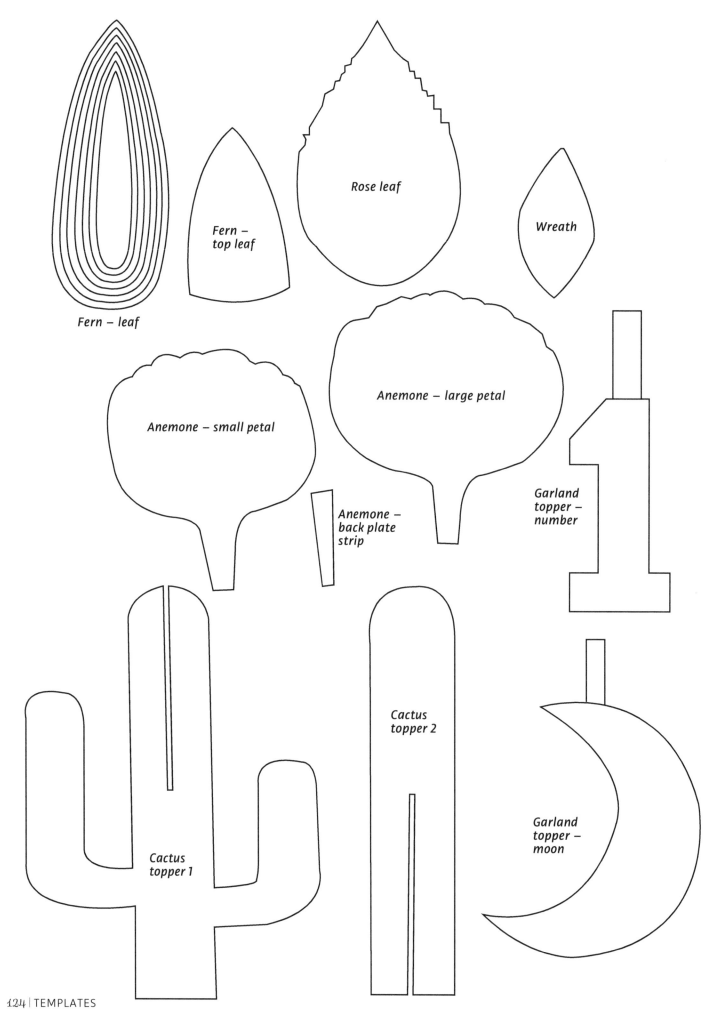

Fern – leaf

Fern – top leaf

Rose leaf

Wreath

Anemone – small petal

Anemone – large petal

Anemone – back plate strip

Garland topper – number

Cactus topper 1

Cactus topper 2

Garland topper – moon

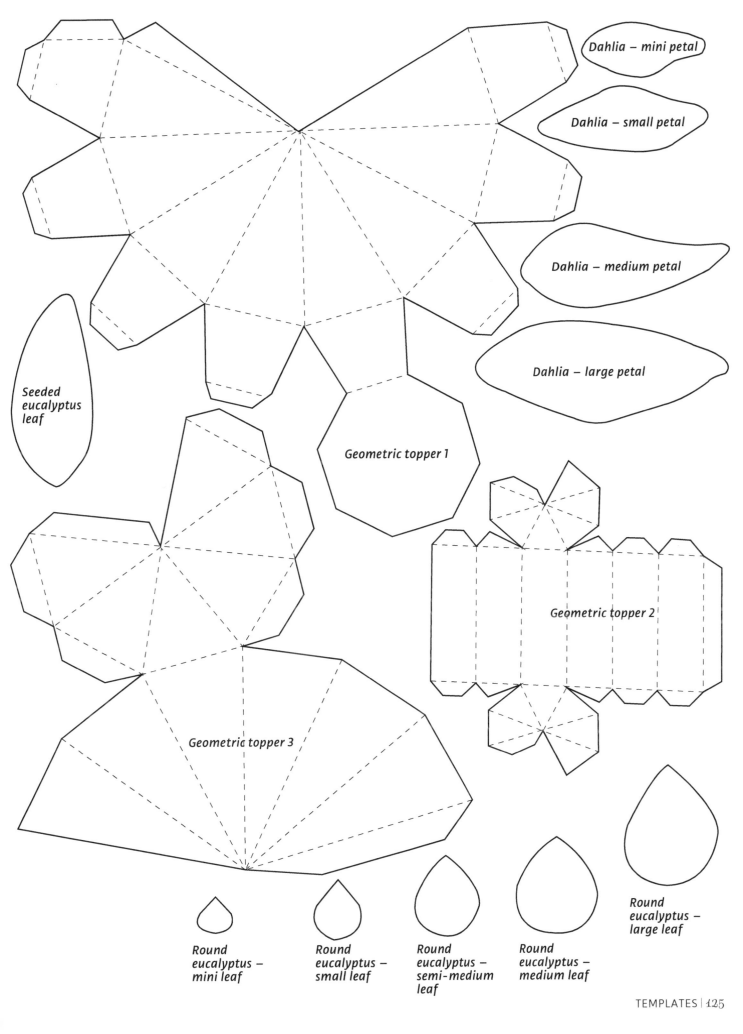

Dahlia – mini petal

Dahlia – small petal

Dahlia – medium petal

Dahlia – large petal

Seeded
eucalyptus
leaf

Geometric topper 1

Geometric topper 2

Geometric topper 3

Round
eucalyptus –
mini leaf

Round
eucalyptus –
small leaf

Round
eucalyptus –
semi-medium
leaf

Round
eucalyptus –
medium leaf

Round
eucalyptus –
large leaf

SUPPLIERS

HEY THERE, CUPCAKE!

Silicone round (petal) molds, printed wafer paper, wafer paper cardstock

www.heythere-cupcake.com

ICING IMAGES

Paper Potion

www.icingimages.com

SMOOTHFOAM

Closed-cell styrofoam balls and cones

www.smoothfoam.com

SWEET STICKS

Edible Art Decorative Paint

www.edibleartpaint.com

SIMI CAKES

Simi isomalt nibs

www.simicakes.com

L.A. GOLD LEAF U.S.

Edible gold leaf

www.lagoldleafus.com

SUGARPASTE

Crystal Colors petal dusts

www.sugarpaste.com

AUI FINE FOODS

Metallic gold dust

www.auifinefoods.com

PETAL CRAFTS

Two-sided silicone leaf veiner

www.petalcrafts.com

JO-ANN STORES

All-over-the-page paper punch

www.joann.com

ABOUT THE AUTHOR

Stevi Auble started her cake career in 2010 with the inception of her San Diego based business, Hey there, Cupcake! A self-taught artist, Stevi focused strongly on the use of wafer paper, a mostly unused medium at the time in the cake industry. Over the past years, she has worked on innovative techniques and methods to transform the unassuming thin sheets into life-like flowers and unique finishes. She is a world-renowned, award-winning artist and instructor, invited to teach at numerous venues around the world, to share her processes and broaden the art form. In doing so, she has helped to bring the use of wafer paper to where it is today: as a staple and readily used medium in the industry. Aside from her wafer paper art innovation, she is known for her modern aesthetic and substantial use of negative space and interesting color combinations within her designs. When not traveling or creating wedding cakes, she loves spending her time with her two daughters and husband, enjoying all that Southern California has to offer – numerous golf courses, the beach, amazing restaurants and Disneyland.

INDEX

A DAVID AND CHARLES BOOK
© David and Charles, Ltd 2017

David and Charles is an imprint of David and Charles, Ltd
Suite A, Tourism House, Pynes Hill, Exeter, EX2 5WS

Text and Designs © Stevi Auble 2017
Layout and Photography © David and Charles, Ltd 2017

First published in the UK and USA in 2017

A catalogue record for this book is available from the
British Library.

ISBN-13: 978-1-4463-0660-4 paperback
ISBN-13: 978-1-4463-7547-1 PDF
ISBN-13: 978-1-4463-7546-4 EPUB

Content Director: Ame Verso
Senior Editor: Jeni Hennah
Project Editor: Jane Trollope
Design Manager: Anna Wade
Designers: Ali Stark and Lorraine Inglis
Photographer: Nathan Rega
Production Manager: Beverley Richardson

David and Charles publishes high-quality books on a wide range of subjects.
For more information visit www.davidandcharles.com.

Share your makes with us on social media using #dandcbooks and follow us
on Facebook and Instagram by searching for @dandcbooks.